FREE YOUR CHILD FROM

ASTHMA

FREE YOUR CHILD FROM
ASTHMA

A Four-Week Plan to Eliminate Symptoms

GARY RACHELEFSKY, M.D.
WITH PATRICIA GARRISON

McGraw·Hill

New York Chicago San Francisco Lisbon London Madrid Mexico City
Milan New Delhi San Juan Seoul Singapore Sydney Toronto

The *McGraw·Hill* Companies

Library of Congress Cataloging-in-Publication Data

Rachelefsky, Gary.
  Free your child from asthma : a four-week plan to eliminate symptoms / by Gary
Rachelefsky with Patricia Garrison.
      p.   cm.
  Includes index.
  ISBN 0-07-145986-3
  1. Asthma in children—popular works.   I. Garrison, Patricia.   II. Title.

  RJ436.A8R33   2007
  618.92′238—dc22   2005021517

1 2 3 4 5 6 7 8 9 0   FGR/FGR   0 9 8 7 6 5

ISBN 0-07-145986-3

Interior design by Rattray Design

McGraw-Hill books are available at special quantity discounts to use as premiums and sales
promotions, or for use in corporate training programs. For more information, please write to the
Director of Special Sales, Professional Publishing, McGraw-Hill, Two Penn Plaza, New York, NY
10121-2298. Or contact your local bookstore.

The information contained in this book is intended to provide helpful and informative material on
the subject addressed. It is not intended to serve as a replacement for professional medical
advice. Any use of the information in this book is at the reader's discretion. The authors and
publisher specifically disclaim any and all liability arising directly or indirectly from the use or
application of any information contained in this book. A health-care professional should be
consulted regarding your specific situation.

This book is printed on acid-free paper.

To Gail, my understanding wife of thirty-nine years, and to my three daughters, two sons-in-law, and five grandchildren (two of whom have asthma)

Contents

Acknowledgments

I WISH TO thank the thousands of children I have cared for with asthma, as it is their determination and spirit that inspired me to write this book. My deepest gratitude also goes to Drs. Charles E. Lewis and Mary Ann Lewis for teaching me how to involve children in their own care and decision making and how to work with families so that they can become educated and empowered regarding the care of their children. I also wish to thank Drs. E. Richard Stiehm and Sheldon Siegel, who introduced me to the field of allergy, asthma, and immunology; I credit them with my becoming a clinician-scientist who remains passionate about helping patients with asthma and allergies.

Introduction

What's Wrong with Your Child's Asthma Care?

"ASTHMA RATES IN children are skyrocketing!" "Asthma Out of Control in America's Kids!" The headlines shout what so many parents already know. Childhood asthma rates are spiraling upward, and millions of children across the country are struggling to breathe.

Asthma is the leading cause of chronic illness in children and the most frequent reason for emergency department visits in those under age five. Symptoms of asthma keep children out of school and parents out of work to care for them. Asthma compromises a child's life, scholastically and socially, hindering her from fully enjoying school and play. Children with asthma often feel they can't do all that they want to do and that other children take for granted. Sports, outdoor pursuits, dance lessons, playing certain musical instruments, and simply being active and having fun are viewed with caution. Children, like their parents, worry that too much activity may provoke an asthma episode.

Meanwhile, as a parent, you feel anxious and overwhelmed, always worrying that an episode is around the corner. Into an already hectic family life, asthma brings stress, exhaustion, guilt, marital and sibling conflict, and the gnawing anxiety that your child may wake up again in the middle of the night terrified and fighting for air. Add to this oppressive mix the frustration that you and millions of parents feel when you take your child to the doctor, follow the treatment plan, and administer the drugs your doctor prescribes, yet still he wheezes, coughs, and experiences frightening episodes that send him to the emergency department, making your family life far less satisfying and promising than it could be. You are not alone. Millions of parents and children live their lives consumed with asthma's problems and unpredictability.

Why I Wrote This Book

As an asthma specialist who has treated thousands of children over the past thirty years, I have never been more concerned about the state of asthma care in the United States than now. Here we sit at the beginning of a new millennium, losing a battle to a disease that has had the benefit of more advances than virtually any other in the twentieth century.

In the early 1970s, it was the promise of a new era in understanding and treatment that drove me to choose as my specialty allergy and immunology with a focus on asthma. I grew excited at the prospect of helping children and their families reap the benefits of what I believed would be an asthma revolution. Just as the 1950s and '60s had seen a growing awareness of asthma as a true medical condition—not the fault of neuroses or bad parenting, as had once been widely believed—the 1970s and '80s would see an explosion of research and new findings that would completely transform our understanding of asthma. We would learn that asthma is not just a disease of airway restriction, but also one of inflammation, and that, left untreated, the inflammation worsens the condition and causes permanent damage.

This new insight produced an avalanche of new medications and treatment approaches that address the underlying inflammation, making it possible to limit the damaging effects of asthma. We, as physicians, knew what we needed to know about our adversary, and we then had better weapons in the medical arsenal with which to fight the battle.

Sadly, the "revolution" never quite made its way to patients. To be sure, there have been improvements in asthma care. But for the most part, the advances in research and treatment have not made an appreciable difference in the lives of patients and their families. Asthma rates continue to spiral upward, and emergency department visits and deaths each year remain unacceptably high.

Why is asthma on the rise, and why, despite our knowledge and insights, are children and their parents still at the mercy of asthma's symptoms? The reasons for asthma increases in children are multifactored and often confusing. Some data blame the environment (both indoor and outdoor), while other findings suggest the culprit is our overfed, sedentary Western lifestyle. Some data say children today are exposed too early to too many bacteria and viruses, while other theories suggest the opposite—children spend too much of their early life stuck indoors in sterile, energy-tight homes. Certainly, more research is needed to get to the bottom of the childhood asthma crisis.

But just as it is important to research the reasons behind childhood asthma, it is equally important to focus our energies on how we treat and prevent asthma. What of the millions of children who end up in the emergency department, time and time again, in life-threatening situations? What of the children who barely control symptoms each day, wheezing, feeling short of breath, unable to do all they want to do? What about the children on many medications or the wrong medications, who suffer unpleasant side effects? What of the parents who dutifully take their child to the doctor yet still don't see measurable, significant improvement? What of children and families who simply can't imagine a life without asthma symptoms?

The Asthma Care Quandary

If you're reading this book, you may be frustrated with the lack of progress in your child's asthma. You're following "doctor's orders" yet seeing no real improvement. You're still worried and anxious as your child continues to wheeze or experiences that familiar nighttime cough, and you're continually preoccupied with the possibility that you and he will again end up in the emergency department in the throes of another life-threatening asthma episode. I call this go-nowhere bind the *asthma care quandary*—a bewildering situation that finds you doing all you're told to do, without a true payoff in progress.

What is at the root of this quandary? In short, the way medicine is currently practiced in the United States. The way health care professionals are trained combined with the time restrictions imposed by managed-care plans makes it virtually impossible for the pediatrician or family practice physician to provide the kind of accurate diagnosis, appropriate care, and comprehensive information and updates that parents need to keep children healthy and virtually symptom-free.

Family physicians and pediatricians currently care for the majority of all asthma patients in the United States. Pediatricians may refer a patient to an asthma specialist, but often they do not, and in some cases, they may be penalized by managed-care companies if they refer too often. As a parent, you may need to fork over higher copays, go through an inconvenient bureaucratic morass of paperwork and forms, or pay all out-of-pocket costs for specialty care, so you may be reluctant to move through the referral process.

Certainly, any physician's job is to do everything possible for a patient, and many children and their families have been helped by my primary-care colleagues. But many family physicians and pediatricians, through no fault of their own, did not receive comprehensive training in asthma and allergic disease in medical school and postgraduate training. Moreover, they treat hundreds of patients each year with a range of varied symptoms and concerns, so they don't see asthma patients all day, every day, as does a specialist.

While this book will not diminish the tireless efforts of many health care professionals involved in asthma care, it will not ignore the fact that their training—to be able to recognize and treat a host of diseases quickly—has not always prepared them for the subtleties of asthma in children. Despite exhaustive attempts to help patients, many health care professionals miss critical clues that can mean the difference between a vital, active, and enjoyable life for a child or one consumed with worry and illness.

In addition to asthma training, many primary-care physicians and pediatricians lack the time to deliver comprehensive asthma education to parents and children. Not only is asthma a complicated disease to diagnose and manage, but it demands active and ongoing involvement of an experienced health care team: asthma educators, nurse practitioners, and even psychologists, to support families in dealing with the emotional, social, academic, and physical aspects of a childhood illness that is chronic, serious, and lifelong. Most pediatricians and family physicians simply don't have the ability to direct such extensive resources against one condition.

Interestingly, studies have shown that family physicians acknowledge that the current health care system finds them treating conditions for which they may have inadequate training. In a 2000 survey published in the *New England Journal of Medicine*, the majority of family physicians admitted to feeling overwhelmed by the demands of a managed-care-dominated medical system that requires them to treat conditions that may be beyond their range of expertise. I believe that asthma is one of these conditions.

Fortunately, efforts are under way—notably the National Asthma Education and Prevention Program of the National Heart, Lung, and Blood Institute and the National Institutes of Health—to address the educational gaps of primary-care training and to give all physicians, pharmacists, school nurses, and other health care professionals a comprehensive and uniform approach to the diagnosis and management of asthma and asthma-related diseases. Numerous professional organizations, including the American Academy of Allergy, Asthma and Immunology, the American College of Allergy, Asthma and Immunology, the American Academy of Family Physicians, the American Academy of Pediatrics, and the National Association of School Nurses, among others, offer intensive continuing medical education programs in asthma.

Still, guidelines and other state-of-the-art management strategies are incorporated inconsistently into medical practice. As a result, there is no assurance that the stipulations in the guidelines are being adopted universally or comprehensively throughout the medical system.

How to Use This Book

Until there is some assurance of the consistency and uniformity of asthma diagnosis and treatment throughout the United States, you as a parent will need to "supplement the system." You and your child can't wait. You want him to begin living a symptom-free life now, and he deserves nothing less.

Consider this book your way out of the asthma care quandary. By the time you have finished reading it, you will have gained a fuller understanding of your child's disease; better control of his asthma symptoms; an awareness of all aspects of the treatment plan; a working knowledge of asthma medications and their benefits and side effects; and an insight into life with asthma now, while he is in school, and in the future. Both of you will be able to enjoy life more fully without unremitting asthma symptoms, and you'll have the confidence to know when things are off course, when he needs help, and often, what kind of help may be needed.

I've written this book to be the practical, simple step-by-step guide to fill the asthma treatment gaps and set you and your child on a course to help shape a vibrant, healthy path together.

FREE YOUR CHILD FROM ASTHMA

PART I

Understanding Asthma Care and Treatment

1

Assessing Current Treatment

Is Your Child Symptom-Free?

MARY AND ROB P. brought their sixteen-month-old daughter to my office after several exasperating weeks of seeing her health go from bad to worse. The baby's nighttime cough and itchy, scaling skin had been diagnosed as eczema—a common allergy-related skin condition in infants that produces intense itching and scaly skin. A food allergy was suspected, and she was placed on a restricted diet. But while the eczema symptoms lessened, the low-calorie diet prevented her from gaining weight, and she failed to thrive. Moreover, her nighttime cough worsened—particularly when she contracted a cold or other upper respiratory infection—and she began having difficulty breathing. The parents took her to another doctor, who accurately diagnosed her with asthma. She was given a quick-acting bronchodilator, which her parents administered each night with the use of a nebulizer (a mechanized inhalation device) to open up her airways when she started to wheeze. But a bronchodilator, such as albuterol, often isn't enough to control the disease and prevent asthma episodes. (I'll discuss this and other asthma devices more in Chapter 4.) As a result, she didn't get better and was simply being kept alive. Patients with asthma, including infants, typically need ongoing treatment as well as immediate relief from a bronchodilator to reduce the airway inflammation that triggers an asthma episode.

When Joan and Harry N. visited my office, they were beside them-selves with worry. Their five-year-old son had been rushed to the emer-gency department fifteen times in one year with asthma episodes, two of which almost killed him, even though he had been taking multiple asthma medications every day for the last two years. They told me they were doing everything right, and I believed them, but I agreed that something was terribly wrong. They had tried to talk to their physi-cian, expressing their concerns over the frequent emergencies. But, they were told that their child had a difficult case and that they would need to expect and deal with emergencies. Unfortunately, his asthma had been completely mismanaged.

No child who is receiving optimum asthma care should end up in the emergency department from an asthma episode, and any emergency department visit is a warning that the child's asthma is not being ade-quately controlled. In the case of Joan and Harry's son, his problems were a failure of his asthma care. After speaking with the parents, I realized that he had not been properly checked for allergies and, in fact, often experienced his asthma episodes following time spent away from home—at day care, grandmother's house, or a friend's birthday party.

After an evaluation, I determined that the boy had an allergy to milk and milk products, so a bite of ice cream, a glass of milk at grandma's, or a piece of cheese could quickly produce uncontrolled asthma symptoms. The answer was not more drugs but fewer, coupled with a restriction on milk and milk products. Within the next four weeks, his parents noticed a complete and welcomed turnaround. He experienced drastically reduced symptoms, requiring only one asthma medication each day. More importantly, he never had to be rushed to the emergency department again with an asthma episode.

Both of these cases point to a disturbing but very real fact: despite reams of data, new medications, and warehouses full of brochures and patient education materials, asthma is notoriously mismanaged throughout the United States. As a complicated, multifactor disease for which many pediatricians and family physicians have received little training, asthma goes underdiagnosed, misdiagnosed, and undertreated with the wrong medications, too many medications, or not enough to get symptoms under control and limit permanent damage to airways and worsening of symptoms over time. As a result, children merely sur-vive, and parents remain in a constant state of worry, with implications that go well beyond their child's health. The stress of asthma—its seeming unpredictability and serious symptoms—can throw an entire household into a state of constant anxiety, wreaking havoc on marriages, relationships with siblings, and family dynamics. Parents often blame themselves and each other for a situation that refuses to improve, while other children feel neglected or equally concerned about the health of their brother or sister. It is, quite frankly, no way to live; more importantly, it is completely unnecessary.

But how do you know if your child is the victim of asthma mismanagement (however well-intentioned the care) or on the right track? How do you know whether your asthma goals for your child are realistic or whether you are settling for the "best you and he can get"? You've been to the doctor, followed the treatment plan, and struggled to give medications, yet symptom improvement seems modest at best. It has been two weeks, and your four-year-old is still coughing, still has episodes of chest tightening, and has little stamina. You are lying awake at night, worried that another asthma episode is looming. You're following doctor's orders, but your child doesn't seem to be getting all that much better. In fact, you ended up in the emergency department again, the same afternoon he had been to a birthday party at another child's home. You thought that those horrific trips to the emergency department, with him struggling to breathe, would now be a thing of the past. But sadly, it appears that they are not.

So you ask yourself whether this is what life with an asthmatic child is all about. Is it a harsh reality that—even under a physician's care—things will never be quite right? Will you always need to anticipate an asthma episode and accept that he will never have the vitality and the energy to do what other children do? Or are you being too impatient? Doesn't improvement take time? And what is improvement, anyway? What do you and your asthmatic child have a right to expect?

These are the questions that haunt parents. They can be incessant and disturbing. You may try to ignore them, but you shouldn't. They are the questions that will—with the help of this book—propel you into action. Far from overreactions or the anxious half thoughts of the nonphysician, these questions and many others, are the building blocks for forming an empowered relationship with your child's asthma doctor, and for transforming your child's life.

Raising Your Asthma IQ

As a parent, you undoubtedly have come to trust your instincts. When your child is unhappy, troubled, or embarrassed, your instincts can often clue you in and help you determine how best to guide him out of a difficult situation or make sure he gets the help he needs. With infants and very young children, instincts and observation are critical, since your little ones cannot tell you what is wrong.

When living with an asthmatic child, your instincts and those nagging suspicions that something isn't quite right can be an invaluable gauge for assessing whether the current treatment approach is adequate and what to do if you feel that he isn't reaching his asthma goals. But they are not enough. You will also need knowledge about asthma. You'll need advice on how to critically observe his symptoms, assess his progress, and gain the skills you need to build a partnership with your physician in the best interest of your child. You'll learn that the questions a doctor asks—or fails to—can often mean the difference between effectively managing your child's asthma or suffering with symptoms day in and day out. You'll know what to do when you suspect that your doctor has overlooked some crucial piece of information or a diagnostic test that can lead to a treatment plan that works and rids your child of the daily burden of asthma symptoms. And you'll get specifics on the kinds of questions you should be asking your physician and other health care professionals to ensure optimum care today and well into the future.

You will receive all of this information and guidance in the upcoming chapters. I will not only increase your asthma IQ, but also pull the curtain on what happens in the doctor's office that keeps your child from getting the help he needs, and give you the power to have an impact on your dealings with your physician concerning your child's asthma goals. However, first you need to have a clear sense of what you're dealing with when it comes to childhood asthma, what you both have a right to expect, and when to suspect that his asthma treatment plan may be off track.

The Childhood Asthma Epidemic

Asthma is one of the most common chronic diseases of childhood, and prevalence continues to skyrocket. An estimated 9 million U.S. children under eighteen have asthma, and 4 million have at least one asthma attack, or episode, each year. Research suggests that only 50 percent have been diagnosed, with some statistics suggesting that millions of children with asthma have been misdiagnosed as having recurrent bronchitis or pneumonia.

Asthma rates in children under age five jumped by more than 160 percent from 1980 to 1994, and recent statistics show no signs of a decrease. Asthma is the third leading cause of preventable hospitalizations in children. Of the more than 1.8 million asthma-related emergency department visits each year, 750,000 involve children. More than 14 million school days are missed each year due to asthma, as well as 14.5 million workdays for their parents. Children with asthma miss more than three times as many days from school as children without.

Asthma knows no racial, ethnic, or gender boundaries. It is prevalent in cities and suburbs, in affluent, middle-class, and poor communities. While rates continue to climb throughout the United States, they are 26 percent higher in African-American children than in white children. The foundations for these discrepancies are complex, but children living in poor, urban environments may have far greater barriers to quality health care than other children while also suffering greater exposure to environmental irritants both inside and outside the home.

The reasons for the sharp increases in childhood asthma in the past twenty years continue to baffle researchers, but several, occasionally conflicting, theories have emerged. Some researchers suggest our squeaky-clean living environments may be a factor. Known as the *hygiene hypothesis*, this theory holds that our airtight, energy-efficient homes, antibacterial obsessions, and efforts to keep kids completely free of dirt and germs render their immune systems less capable of dealing with symptom inducers—such as allergens (pollen, pet dander, dust mites) and irritants (smoke, temperature changes)—that they ultimately face when they are exposed to the wider world of day care and preschool. Still, other data essentially say the reverse: that exposure to bacteria and viruses from other children in day care and preschool predisposes children to asthma. Meanwhile, researchers are exploring the link between childhood obesity and rising childhood asthma rates. These studies, like many others, are highly inconclusive, requiring much additional research before their results are proven as fact.

The Good News About Asthma Treatment

However, while it is true that asthma rates are worsening, it is also true that the disease and its symptoms are far easier to treat and control today than in years past. More than three decades of intensive research and discoveries about childhood asthma have expanded our understanding of the disease and have led to the development of safe and effective treatments and patient care strategies that can so minimize asthma symptoms that they are, at most, nothing more than an occasional, minor nuisance.

We now know, for example, that asthma is a multifaceted disease that both constricts the airways of the lungs and promotes airway inflammation. This combination of airway constriction and inflammation causes the coughing, wheezing, chest tightening, and shortness of breath that are the hallmarks of asthma and, if left untreated, may eventually lead to permanent damage of the airways. Research has shown us that the inflammation of the airways is what causes permanent airway damage and makes asthma symptoms worse and more difficult to control. Current treatments tackle asthma on both fronts: they open up restricted airways so that a child can breathe, and they reduce the inflammation that prompts the airway constriction and damages the linings of the airways. Modern treatments not only manage symptoms but also reverse the progression of the disease over time. These treatment strategies can eliminate asthma episodes as well as make emergency department visits for asthma a thing of the past. They can enable children and their parents to take control of asthma, rather than allowing the disease to determine the day-to-day family routine, hobbies, interests, extracurricular activities, and academic choices, as well as how a child feels about himself.

Children who have been receiving proper asthma care won't need to be rushed to the hospital or to their doctor's office with an asthma-related emergency. They experience virtually no symptoms and need very little asthma medication to breathe freely and feel healthy. You won't hear them constantly wheezing or coughing throughout the night. Babies will breathe normally, feed without struggle, and respond to parents with animation and excitement. Older children will have the energy to run and play, without coughing, shortness of breath, wheezing, or undue fatigue. They won't need to avoid an activity they want to do—whether it's soccer, dance classes, or clarinet lessons. If they are over age eight, or around the third grade, they can be taught about their asthma and appreciate that it is chronic and requires attention, but know that it does not need to intrude on their life, activities, or plans. They feel in control of asthma and aren't worried that another episode might be on the horizon.

Why Your Child—and You—Are in the Bind You're In

Sadly, millions of children and their parents are far from living the symptom-free life. To be sure, they are following doctor's orders, but they still experience frequent asthma symptoms and episodes. These are the patients I often see in my practice, brought in by frustrated and exhausted parents, who don't understand why their child is not showing significant improvement.

In the introduction, I outlined my own frustrations with the medical profession. My colleagues are well-meaning, careful professionals who want to do all they can for their patients. But the current medical system, combined with the complexity of childhood asthma diagnosis and management, has conspired to undermine asthma care for millions of children in the United States, virtually denying them the symptom-free life they are entitled to. Pediatricians and family practice physicians, who see more than 75 percent of all childhood asthma cases in the United States, are often poorly trained to recognize asthma symptoms in children or to adequately manage symptoms over time. Asthma is chronic and complicated, and asthma clues can be subtle, mimicking other diseases and conditions.

Given their age and lack of perspective, children may underplay or be unable to communicate how they are feeling, leading parents and physicians to underestimate the impact of symptoms on their child's well-being. Moreover, asthma is not a simple disease to manage; attention must be paid to asthma "triggers"—from cat dander to certain foods—that can set off symptoms or a full-blown episode, as well as a finely tuned sense of when your child may be headed for asthma trouble. (I discuss this more in Chapter 7.) Parents and children must keep track of a medication regimen, know how to administer a variety of drugs at different times of day, and be able to negotiate asthma care at school, day care, summer camps, and after-school clubs. A family physician may lack the resources to devote to helping parents effectively manage and monitor asthma at home, day care, and school.

Adding to the conundrum are the roadblocks in many patient-physician relationships. Too often, the patient-physician dynamic undermines your ability to find out all you need to know and to openly question a physician's decisions. Patients, and parents in particular, are often passive in their dealings with physicians. As a doctor, I understand that, as clinicians, we have done much to cultivate this passivity. We are trained to be in control, and we may have difficulty sharing any control with patients.

Moreover, we have had little training in actively listening to patients, hearing what they have to say, watching for nonverbal clues even if they aren't saying anything, and engaging them in becoming active partners in their child's asthma care. Like anyone else, we avoid what it is we aren't good at. Couple this lack of listening skill with the minimal training that pediatricians and family physicians receive in childhood asthma care, and we have a recipe for trouble.

The answer? Asthma care needs to be supplemented with active, informed input from parents and caregivers—what I call *proactive asthma care*. Parents can have a dramatic impact on asthma care for their children, asserting themselves and insisting that the medical profession carefully, thoughtfully, and methodically make use of all that is available in asthma treatment today, while recognizing when referral to a specialist or another physician may be necessary.

It does not mean that you need to switch health care professionals or risk a confrontation with the office nurse. What it does mean is that you will be in the lead along with your doctor in making sure that your child receives the best care possible and that you have all that you need to safeguard your child's health at home, at school or day care, and during extracurricular activities.

Common Asthma Missteps

I cannot overemphasize the gap between what we know about asthma and have at our disposal and how asthma is often treated in the physician's office. What often fills the gap are common "missteps" and misdiagnoses that are at the root of asthma trouble for millions of children. These mistakes are problematic in that they set the stage for treatment, which may be inadequate as a result, while failing to give you all the information you need to be an active partner in your child's care. You therefore can't be as effective in changing the situation or addressing the mistake, because you simply lack sufficient information with which to move forward. Here are some common asthma mistakes that keep children from getting all the help they need.

Misdiagnosing Asthma

Infants and children with asthma may be misdiagnosed with a cough or bad cold and sent home with a prescription for cough medicine. The cold may linger for weeks, and still parents are told that their child has a bad cold or viral infection that will eventually go away. Meanwhile, the child is at risk for an asthma episode.

Children and infants with asthma are also often misdiagnosed with pneumonia or bronchitis. Then they are treated with drugs and approaches that do nothing to begin addressing asthma symptoms.

In addition, children with a persistent wheeze may be misdiagnosed with viral upper respiratory infections. While it is true that infants and young children can have wheezing episodes and not have asthma, asthma must be suspected if a child has more than two wheezing episodes associated with upper respiratory infections.

Ignoring the Asthma/Allergy Connection

Remember Mary and Rob P.'s sixteen-month-old daughter from the beginning of the chapter? Parents of children with eczema are often told that their child has a food allergy, period. While the child may have a food allergy, eczema is a risk factor for future asthma. Did the doctor ask about wheezing, nighttime coughing, and difficulty feeding? These are asthma symptoms but are frequently misinterpreted as related to a food allergy when a young child has eczema. Food allergy is, in my opinion, overdiagnosed in babies and young toddlers, often with serious consequences. Food allergy may coexist with asthma, but it is not at all helpful to diagnose a food allergy without suspecting asthma. If certain vitamins or foods are eliminated in the name of a nonexistent food allergy, children may not receive the nutrients they need and may fail to thrive. Meanwhile, the asthma is not being treated, leaving children vulnerable to asthma symptoms and episodes.

The allergy-asthma connection is overlooked. Babies who are diagnosed with eczema (an itchy, scaly skin condition) and other allergies are at serious risk of developing asthma. Failure to be on the watch for asthma can keep young children from getting help early. If allergies have not been investigated and are not properly controlled, then I can virtually guarantee that a child's asthma will not improve.

Why are allergy tests overlooked? With only cursory training in allergic disease, pediatricians and family practice physicians often underestimate the influence of allergies in childhood asthma. In addition, many pediatricians believe that allergy testing is not worthwhile in children under the age of five and will produce false negatives, so they don't recommend doing the tests. In truth, allergy testing can be very useful in young children and may help identify environmental (indoor/outdoor) or food allergens.

Allergy testing is done as a blood test or a skin test, the latter always performed by an allergy specialist who has the expertise to administer and interpret the results. While not all children with allergies develop asthma, it is a primary risk factor for the disease in children. Allergies and asthma are the most frequently reported pair of chronic illnesses in children under age eighteen. In fact, studies have shown that 90 percent of children and 70 percent of adolescents who have asthma also suffer with allergies. In a clear example of how data do not always inform medical practice, research abounds on the strong relationship between asthma and allergies in children, yet I have treated thousands of children whose parents are surprised to find that their child's asthma is driven by allergies. Once we treat the allergies, the asthma symptoms usually improve dramatically.

Not Getting the Right Information

Parents are given confusing instructions and sketchy information about their child's disease and treatments. With an asthma diagnosis often come a fistful of prescriptions and a hurried review of how to administer asthma medications, but parents often leave the physician's office with virtually no understanding of the disease, their child's asthma triggers (what sets off wheezing or an episode), or how to avoid them. For example, you may have been given a prescription for a *bronchodilator* (a drug that opens constricted airways when a child is short of breath) given through an *inhaler* (a handheld device that delivers the drug into the lungs) with a spacer or holding chamber attached, but you may not have been given enough guidance to feel confident that you are using the device properly so that your child can get the appropriate amount of medication into his lungs. You may have been given too many drugs or not enough. In the case of an infant, you may have been instructed to deliver asthma medication through a *nebulizer* (an air compressor that produces a fine mist of medication) that is often used for young children and babies who are unable to use an inhaler. But as I mentioned earlier in the chapter, bronchodilators, whether given through an inhaler or a nebulizer to open restricted airways, do nothing to treat the airway inflammation. Anti-inflammatory drugs may actually prevent or reverse permanent lung damage. I will review the difference between bronchoconstriction and inflammation and their role in childhood asthma in Chapter 2, but suffice it to say, children often receive inadequate treatment—with medication that opens constricted airways when they are struggling to breathe but does nothing to treat the condition over the long term.

In addition, parents are often given inadequate guidance and insight into what causes asthma and what may set off an asthma episode in their child. As we've discussed, allergens can trigger an asthma episode. In addition, irritants such as cigarette smoke, exhaust fumes, cleaners, and other factors such as crying, laughing, and weather changes are common asthma triggers, but parents can't be expected to manage them if they don't know what they are.

Insufficient attention is paid to the whole of a child's life, and parents are given little guidance on how to manage their child's asthma away from home. Educators, school nurses, day-care workers, physical education teachers, and others involved in his life need to know about his asthma and be informed on what to do if he needs medications or if problems arise. (I cover this in week three with a school asthma management plan in Chapter 8.) You need to know how to handle potentially complicated or difficult issues that could arise in dual-living arrangements, as in the case of divorced and separated parents (Chapter 6) or when traveling, during play dates at other children's homes, at sleepovers and birthday parties, and in other aspects of his life that take him out of the house (Chapter 8). Asthma episodes can happen anywhere. But unfortunately, physicians and other health care professionals may never address these issues unless you initiate the conversation.

In short, many parents who receive an asthma diagnosis for their child are given only enough to keep him functioning and nothing to eliminate symptoms and ensure that he thrives. You may be one of them, and as an asthma specialist, I can tell you that both you and your child are entitled to much more.

So, should a child under a physician's care still be experiencing nighttime cough? Should he be rushed to the emergency department with an asthma episode? Should you be riddled with anxiety about his condition? Should you be unsure how to approach school and day care about his condition and day-to-day health care needs? The answer to all of these questions is no. These concerns and problems all point to gaps in diagnosis, overlooked asthma triggers, or information for you and your child in moving forward with an effective asthma treatment plan. The wrong medications may have been prescribed, there may be difficulties with administering them with asthma devices, or they may be inadequate to successfully treat his symptoms. Whatever the problem, whatever the mistakes or misinterpretations, you as a parent—along with your child—have the ability to improve the situation and get him on a track toward true asthma progress.

How to Measure Progress: The Childhood Asthma Bill of Rights

What do you and your child have a right to expect from asthma treatment? Here is the yardstick by which we should measure progress: **If your child is not enjoying a virtually symptom-free life within four weeks of first receiving an asthma diagnosis, then you may be dealing with a situation in need of better asthma care.** It doesn't necessarily mean you need to switch physicians, but it does mean that you need to proactively work with your health care professional to accelerate symptom improvement.

While every child and each situation is different, we should measure progress with what I call the *Childhood Asthma Bill of Rights*:

- Elimination of severe or persistent asthma symptoms day and night in *three to four weeks* after beginning treatment
- Mild symptoms (occasional cough and infrequent wheeze) no more than two days per week
- No emergency department visits or hospitalizations
- Few, if any, drug side effects
- Ongoing reduction in the amount of drugs needed to maintain symptom control
- No limitations on activities, including sports
- No missed school days from asthma symptoms
- Knowledge and guidance to manage your child's disease in age-appropriate stages

If you haven't achieved these goals within about one month's time, then the care is inadequate and should be reassessed.

This book will serve as your blueprint for breaking out of the asthma care bind and charting a healthy future for your child. In addition to getting the tools you need to be an active partner in proactive asthma care, you'll also learn the following from this book:

- What an asthma diagnosis means for your child and your family, and what it doesn't
- A comprehensive review of asthma medications and devices, how they work, side effects, and how they need to be administered—We'll review how to use and read a peak-flow meter to monitor his lung function; administer medications to young children; work with school nurses, coaches, camp counselors, troop leaders, and others who supervise and make sure he is safe away from home; travel with medication; and streamline medication plans for divorced and separated parents and working parents.
- What to do when he doesn't get better despite following a treatment plan and avoiding asthma triggers
- How to separate asthma myth from fact

- Real-life issues for children at any age, from managing asthma in an uncooperative preschooler to making a difference with teenagers who may be depressed or embarrassed about their condition—We'll also cover the complicated but routinely overlooked dilemmas of traveling with asthma, managing asthma in college, professional and occupational decisions for your teenager, and managing asthma's changes at menstruation.
- How to raise an empowered patient, making sure he has the practical skills, knowledge, and sense of empowerment to effectively manage asthma throughout his life

With this new approach, you, your child, and your family can look forward to a life where asthma is no longer center stage. You will rid yourself of the anxiety of unanswered questions and unnerving concerns. You will be pivotal in changing the course of his disease and charting a positive course for the future.

2

Asthma Basics

What You Need to Know

WHILE WE TEND to think of it as a modern-day disease, asthma has been plaguing people for centuries. The word *asthma*, which means "labored breathing" in Greek, was mentioned in Homer's *Iliad*, and the Greek physician Hippocrates described asthma symptoms three thousand years ago. Moses Maimonides, a twelfth-century physician, recorded in his patient journal that he "had no magic cure to report" and that asthma should be treated symptomatically. Back then, treatments ranged from giving patients owl's blood mixed with wine to the ever-popular chicken soup.

By the seventeenth and eighteenth centuries, physicians began to understand that asthma results from airway constriction, but effective treatments would be many, many years away. Just as today, asthma was ubiquitous, afflicting the anonymous as well as the rich and famous. In fact, the work of some of history's greatest artists reveals their struggles with asthma. Charles Dickens's autobiographical *David Copperfield* features an asthmatic character, Mr. Omer. Beethoven, who suffered from severe, debilitating asthma, composed his brilliant, turbulent symphonies while railing against the doctors who could not help him. And more recent concertgoers can recall hearing conductor Leonard Bernstein's wheeze above the orchestra during performances.

It was not until the mid-twentieth century that physicians had any treatments approaching effectiveness. Theophylline and ephedrine, introduced in the 1950s, were the first bronchodilators, treating symptoms by opening up constricted airways. More advanced treatments, providing symptom relief and fewer drug side effects, followed in the 1960s and 1970s, but it would take several more years before an understanding of the underlying factors that caused a person's airways to spasm and narrow would emerge, leading to the more effective treatments we have today.

Asthma Clues and Causes

By the 1970s and early '80s, researchers were coming to grips with important findings that would enable physicians not only to treat symptoms, but also to focus on what was happening in a child's airways that prompted repeated episodes of wheezing, breathlessness, coughing, and chest tightness.

Up until the 1970s, researchers and clinicians believed that asthma was a disease caused by constriction alone. This airway constriction was provoked by airway *hyperresponsiveness*, a kind of hypersensitivity that would cause the bronchial tubes to constrict and spasm when exposed to an asthma trigger, such as pollen, smoke, fumes, cat dander, exercise, or emotional upset. Efforts were made to keep children and asthma triggers as far away from each other as possible. Children with asthma were often kept indoors or were forbidden from engaging in any vigorous activity or play. Because asthma episodes were occasionally preceded by an emotional event—such as laughing, crying, or excitement—asthma was believed to have a psychological component. As late as the 1950s, many people believed that asthma was a psychosomatic disorder, that is, "all in one's head." Such nonsense often relegated asthmatic children to special camps and residential treatment centers, where they were isolated from other children and stigmatized. This stigmatization continues to a much lesser degree even today, but old-fashioned notions that children are weak or troubled still bubble under society's surface. (I'll discuss this stigma further in Chapter 3 and ways to handle it in school and other situations in Chapter 8.)

With asthma rates in children rising through the mid-twentieth century in most developed countries, physicians and health care professionals had all they could do to treat symptoms and keep asthmatic children functioning. While physicians attempted to manage and minimize asthma symptoms, researchers continued to ask questions. For example, what causes the airways of some children to spasm when they inhale pollen or cat dander while others might cough or sneeze but continue to breathe normally; and what, if anything, can be done about it?

Airway Inflammation: An Important Discovery

Researchers uncovered the answer to asthma in 1978 with the discovery that the disease was caused by airway inflammation—an inflammation that is chronic and damaging. Irritated and inflamed airways are vulnerable and sensitive to any trigger or irritant. So when a child with asthma is exposed to a trigger, the airways overreact and constrict, producing excess mucus and swelling, which further narrows the airways and increases inflammation. The inflamed and irritated airways are now more likely to overreact again and again, thus contributing to a vicious cycle of inflammation, hyperresponsiveness, and bronchoconstriction. Physicians call this cycle the *inflammatory response*, but parents and children experience it in the unremitting symptoms that produce shortness of breath, chest tightening, coughing and wheezing, and the episodes that keep them locked in asthma's grip.

Bridging the Asthma Gap

Although some physicians and health care professionals still tend to question the importance of inflammation in asthma, the discovery thirty years ago dramatically changed how asthma was viewed by the medical community. It prompted an avalanche of research and new findings that would usher in an asthma revolution, transforming the disease from one that put sufferers at the mercy of unpredictable asthma episodes—remedied only by bronchodilators and other so-called rescue medications—to one in which patients could have more control over their condition and their lives. As I have said earlier, the role of this book is to bridge the gap between this pivotal discovery and the day-to-day management of your child's asthma.

However, for you to fully appreciate the importance of the discovery and its impact on your child's life, we first need to review the basics of childhood asthma and what it does to airways and lung function. Armed with this knowledge, you can better understand your child's disease and treatment, and be better equipped to participate proactively in your child's care.

What Is Happening in Your Child's Lungs?

When lungs are working as they should, we need barely give them a second thought. These two spongy sacs located in the chest cavity do their job efficiently and automatically, taking in enough fresh, oxygen-enriched air to enable cells to work so that our bodies can do what we want and need them to do, and expelling carbon dioxide, a natural by-product of our metabolisms that needs to be removed.

We breathe through our nose and mouth (breathing through the nose is far better for children with asthma, as air is colder and drier when taken in through the mouth, thereby instigating an asthma episode). The air is warmed as its moves through our airways, beginning with the *trachea*, or windpipe, through to the bronchial tubes, located in either lung. The tubes resemble the branches of a tree, with the larger called *bronchi* and the smaller *bronchioles*. The outside lining of the bronchial tubes is made of smooth muscle that expands, or dilates, as we inhale, and constricts when we exhale to push air out of the lungs. At the end of the smaller branches are tiny air sacs, or *alveoli*, surrounded by a network of small blood vessels. It is in these blood vessels that the exchange of gases takes place, with oxygen being absorbed into the bloodstream and carbon dioxide being removed as it exits through our exhalation. It is a process that happens automatically and effortlessly, unless you have asthma.

For asthmatic children, this intricate and complicated series of activities is undermined, making it extremely difficult to get enough air into the lungs, as shown in Figure 2.1. When inflamed airways overreact, they constrict. Airflow is limited, and symptoms begin. In children, one of the chief culprits in setting off asthma symptoms is the immune system. You may ask what the immune system has to do with all of this. Immunity is typically understood as a good thing, as it is our immune systems that respond when we get a bacterial infection, a cut or bruise, or a virus. When our bodies are invaded by a foreign microorganism—a virus or bacteria, for example—the immune sys-

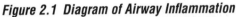

Figure 2.1 Diagram of Airway Inflammation

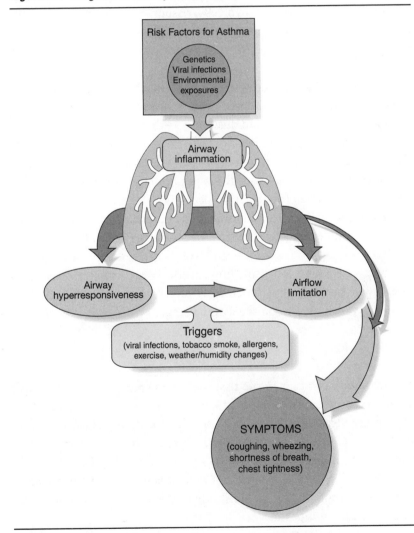

tem goes into high gear, recognizing the invader for the troublemaker that it is and releasing antibodies to destroy the offending bacteria and viruses and get you well again. As the body's chief defender, the immune system responds to any perceived threat by mobilizing the body's resources. Without its vigilance, we simply could not survive.

But the immune system can also malfunction. There are numerous diseases and disorders caused by a faulty immune system. Some, known as autoimmune diseases, occur when the body is unable to distinguish an outside invader from its own cells, tissues, and processes—literally producing antibodies against itself. Multiple sclerosis, lupus erythematosus, psoriasis, and rheumatoid arthritis are examples of autoimmune diseases.

In asthma, the immune system isn't so much confused as alarmist. It works too well against asthma triggers, or *antigens*—such as pollen, cat dander, certain foods, and dust mites—that may be unpleasant but pose no immediate danger. Rather than brush off the dander or pollen with a quick sneeze, the immune system goes into overdrive, mobilizing the body to unleash a cascade of specific antigen-fighting antibodies and setting the stage for an asthma episode.

The immune system is elaborate and complex, but the process that produces and perpetuates asthma symptoms is worth understanding, so that you can better understand your child's condition, why her immune system overreacts, and how an effective asthma treatment plan interrupts the damaging process. Take a look at the following key immune system players on the asthma stage.

Mast Cells

You will find mast cells in the tissues that line parts of the body, such as the nasal passages, airways, throat, sinus cavities, skin, and gastrointestinal tract. Owing to their strategic location and their proximity to blood vessels and mucous membranes, these cells are the first contact for an allergen or trigger. On their own, they pose no problems. However, they have a mother lode of sites on their surfaces that serve as receptors of *IgE*, an antibody that is one of the key perpetrators of asthma symptoms.

IgE

The IgE antibodies sound the clarion call for the cascade of asthma symptoms that leave a child gasping for breath. Children and adults without allergies or asthma make very little IgE, but children with allergic disorders, including asthma, produce high levels of the antibody. This oversupply contributes to the reaction to pollen, cat dander, dust mites, and other relatively harmless substances that don't bother other children. Once the IgE antibodies are mobilized, they unleash histamine, leukotriene, and other potent chemicals, known as *mediators*, that wreak general havoc with the respiratory system, producing the classic "allergic" responses: excess mucus production, runny nose, watery eyes, coughing, itching, and hives—and for children with asthma, airway constriction. IgE antibodies are often the primary culprit in children who develop asthma after age three.

Eosinophils

Certain white blood cells called *eosinophils*, which are directed by lymphocytes, are highly drawn to an asthma reaction, and their attraction to the site only worsens the problem. Eosinophils release more chemicals and enzymes that cause inflammation and tissue damage and, over time, play a pivotal role in *airway remodeling*, which is the name physicians give to the permanent damage caused by untreated, unchecked inflammation.

Identifying Asthma Triggers

The majority of childhood asthma cases are *allergic* asthma, meaning the triggers that set off this damaging process are typically allergens. But in asthma, triggers can also be of the nonallergic variety, such as the common cold, smoke, fumes, exercise, emotional expression (from anger to laughing), exposure to cold air, and changes in weather and humidity. And while uncommon in childhood asthma, there may be no allergies at all.

Typically, children with asthma are vulnerable to a mixed bag of triggers (listed in Table 2.1), and regardless of what sets off the asthma, its course in the airways is the same: inflammation, hyperresponsiveness, constriction, and if untreated, permanent airway damage.

Now you have a basic idea of what is happening in her airways. You know that your asthmatic child possesses more of the antibodies that are at the foundation of asthma symptoms, and that the immune system, as a result, overreacts to harmless stimuli, leaving her with a chronic inflammatory disease with significant lower respiratory symptoms.

But you may now be asking yourself, "Why my child?" Researchers are still unsure why some children develop asthma and others do

Table 2.1 Common Asthma Triggers

Type	Trigger
Allergic triggers	Tree, weed, and grass pollens
	Mold spores
	Animal dander (from cats, dogs, and other furry pets)
	House dust mites
	Cockroach allergens
	Food allergens (most commonly eggs, milk, soy, peanuts, and wheat)
Respiratory viral infections	Bronchitis/bronchiolitis
	Influenza (flu)
	Common colds
Nonallergic triggers (irritants)	Tobacco smoke, wood smoke (from fireplaces)
	Fumes (from paints, chemicals)
	Household and cosmetic products (including strong perfumes, soaps, cleaners, and sprays)
	Chalk dust
	Weather changes (including changes in humidity) and cold air
	Exercise
	Strong emotional responses (laughing, crying)
Undiagnosed or untreated asthma-related disorders	Allergic rhinitis (hay fever)
	Gastroesophageal reflux disease (GERD)
	Sinusitis

not, but they do have enough data to identify which children are more likely than others to be asthmatic.

Genetics: An Important Factor

The causes of asthma can often be found right at home. Asthma is a disease caused by genetic and environmental factors. Typically, a child with asthma inherits a gene for the disease from one or both parents, leaving the child predisposed to developing the disease over time. The gene is often passed from parents or grandparents who have asthma, allergies, or both. Either the parents or the grandparents, or all of you, may have asthma or a history of allergies. Inheriting the gene for asthma, not surprisingly, sharply increases your child's risk of disease.

- If one parent (particularly the mother) has asthma, your child stands a 40 percent increased risk of developing asthma.
- If two parents are asthmatic, the risk jumps to 60 percent.

But, researchers believe that inheriting an asthma gene is only one piece of the picture. Genetics make a child more susceptible, but other critical factors have heightened her risk. The following sections discuss the most common predictors of asthma in children with an inherited susceptibility.

Atopy: Prone to Developing Allergies

The unusual word *atopy* is what physicians use to describe a patient who has the ability to develop IgE antibodies against allergens. Nearly 90 percent of children who develop asthma are *atopic*, meaning they began early on to develop allergies to any number of things—food, pollen, dander. Children who have been diagnosed with eczema, food allergies, or hay fever—particularly in their first years of life—have a greater risk of developing asthma. We also know that IgE, the antibody responsible for the overreaction to allergy triggers, is elevated in children with asthma. Allergies and asthma in children are so closely linked that asthma specialists have a name for the progression of diagnoses from eczema in infancy to hay fever to asthma: the *atopic march*.

Respiratory Tract Infections: Greater Risk for Asthma

A history of viral respiratory tract infections, including bronchiolitis due to *respiratory syncytial virus (RSV)*, in infancy and early childhood puts a child at greater risk for developing asthma. You may have noticed that, following these infections, your child developed a wheezing sound that persisted even when she was no longer sick. You may have raised the issue of wheezing with your pediatrician and may have been told that it would diminish over time. Perhaps it did, only to return with the next viral infection.

Wheezing is a confounding factor in the development of childhood asthma, often confusing physicians as well as parents. Why? Because virtually all children experience a period of wheezing in early childhood, and many do not go on to develop asthma. Asthma specialists hold to a rule of thumb that wheezing should not automatically be suspected as asthma-related until it happens three times—and especially when not associated with a respiratory infection. Unfortunately, many physicians may miss this third-time clue and continue to prescribe cough medicine or other medications in children who have experienced three or more wheezing episodes.

The Role of Gender

While asthma can be equally serious in boys and girls, boys are more likely to develop it. In children under age fourteen, boys with asthma outnumber girls two to one. Boys are born with smaller lung capacity, leaving them with lower rates of airflow into the lungs and with a greater risk of respiratory infections early in life. And as just mentioned, respiratory infections in early life are risk factors for developing asthma.

Environmental Factors

When we think about the environment, we tend to think of air and water quality, but researchers define environment as factors that are present in a child's home, day care, and surroundings that can set the stage for asthma. What are the most common environmental triggers in asthma?

- **Indoor air pollutants:** These include smoke from fireplaces, wood-burning stoves, and tobacco smoke, as well as indoor allergens, such as cockroaches, molds, house dust mites, and animal dander.
- **Outdoor air pollutants:** These include things such as ozone, fossil fuels, and chemicals.

Research points to some progress on limiting children's exposure to environmental risks. According to recent studies from the U.S. Environmental Protection Agency, the number of children whose blood levels showed exposure to secondhand smoke declined between 1988 and 2000. However, rates of asthma in children jumped by more than 160 percent during that same time, underscoring that much more work needs to be done in reducing the risk of both outdoor and indoor pollutants.

Most environmental factors related to asthma are beyond our direct control. It is virtually impossible to control exposure to tree, grass, and weed pollens, for example, and feeling any degree of parental guilt is unnecessary. The regulation of air pollution and issues regarding the use of fossil fuels, pesticides, and ozone depletion require action at the state and federal levels of government. As a parent of a child with asthma, you may want to track these issues and stay abreast of new developments that may have an impact on her health. You can exercise your power through voting, letter writing, and working with asthma groups that advocate for patients' rights. (For some places to start, see the Resources section at the end of the book.)

But nowhere is the power to control a serious asthma risk factor more obvious than in the home. You and others in the family can control whether you smoke, have a furry pet, or use pesticides on your lawn or landscaping and where and how you use other irritants, such as perfumes, household cleaners, and chemicals. The impact of environmental irritants, particularly smoking, can be seen before birth. Research shows that the odds of a child developing asthma symptoms in early life are greatly increased if the mother smoked during pregnancy. Of course, the risk of developing asthma is only compounded if the mother or other household members smoke in the house after the child is born.

Making difficult but definitive decisions around risk factor management will be the focus of Chapter 7, but it is important to know that many asthma triggers are within our control and that we have the power to shape an environment that supports our children's health and well-being.

Medications

If your child has had a reaction to a prescription or over-the-counter drug, that drug could produce a severe asthma episode in the future. This problem occurs in a very small minority, however; in less than 1 percent of asthma cases in children, it is a factor. Certain anti-inflammatory products, such as ibuprofen and aspirin products, can induce a near-fatal asthma episode and must be avoided. Aceta-minophen (Tylenol) is generally considered a safe alternative when you need a fever or pain reducer.

Conditions That Aggravate Asthma

Genetics, gender, and environment aside, other real-world factors can aggravate a child's condition and leave her vulnerable to unchecked asthma. Children with asthma are often underdiagnosed, and when asthma-related conditions are left unchecked, they worsen the asthma or, at the very least, keep a child from getting better. I will review the signs of improperly treated asthma and what is to be done about it in later chapters. For now, here are some of the common conditions that are often undiagnosed and hinder a child's improvement.

Nasal Allergy: When It's More than a Persistent Cold

Despite reams of research and a strong correlation between asthma and allergies in children, many children with a persistent "cold" are never diagnosed for allergic rhinitis, the medical term for hay fever or upper respiratory allergies. Since many physicians overlook the connection between asthma and nasal allergies, it isn't surprising that the conditions resulting from them are overlooked as well. However, nasal allergies can inflame and irritate the upper respiratory system—the nasal passages, sinuses, and upper airways—contributing to the lower-airway hyperresponsiveness we know precipitates an asthma episode.

As a parent, you may have suspected nasal allergies in your child. In retrospect, the symptoms may be obvious. A runny or constantly congested nose, itchy and watering eyes, repeated sneezing—all without fever and persisting for weeks on end—virtually guarantees that the symptoms are not a cold. You may notice that symptoms get worse in the spring and fall, when trees, grasses, and weeds are blooming and releasing pollen into the air, or you may notice that she has tearing, red eyes after being in a house with pets. A blood test or an appropriately done skin test performed by an allergy specialist can detect allergies that are causing her asthma. Antihistamines and other medicines can treat them, along with environmental controls (such as removing the family pet, if necessary) and *immunotherapy* (or allergy shots). If you suspect allergies have not been diagnosed, you must discuss this with your physician right away. I will explain the steps you can take to ensure that she receives appropriate allergy testing in Chapter 9.

Sinusitis: Commonly Overlooked

A close cousin to nasal allergies, *sinusitis*, an inflammation of the sinuses, is common in childhood yet routinely overlooked. Until recently, many physicians believed that the immature nasal cavities of young children made it impossible for them to develop sinusitis, but we now know that this condition can be found in children as young as age one or two. Sinusitis in children typically follows a cold or upper respiratory infection, or goes along with untreated nasal allergies. Their inflamed nasal passages make it difficult for sinuses to drain. As a result, mucus lingers there and becomes a virtual petri dish of bacteria and a breeding ground for infections.

Untreated sinusitis is particularly problematic for children with asthma, as it often provokes symptoms. Researchers aren't sure why, but they suspect that the mucus in the sinuses either backs up and works its way into the bronchial tubes, irritating and further inflaming the airways, or that the inflammation of the sinuses somehow reflexively irritates the airways, leading to symptoms. Making sure that your child is checked for sinusitis and treated appropriately can not only help her feel better, but also reduce the severity of her asthma symptoms.

Gastroesophageal Reflux Disease (GERD)

Often described as severe heartburn, and a major asthma trigger in adults, gastroesophageal reflux disease (GERD) can also affect children. It happens when the valve between the esophagus and the stomach malfunctions, causing stomach acid and undigested food to flow back into the esophagus. The irritation of the esophagus aggravates airway inflammation and contributes to the severity of asthma symptoms if left untreated. If your child typically experiences asthma symptoms at night and complains of a burning or pressure in the middle of the chest, she may have GERD.

Understanding the underlying basis of your child's asthma, why she was predisposed, and what factors can worsen symptoms if not quickly addressed can arm you with the foundation of knowledge you will need to be an active partner in her care. In upcoming chapters, I will discuss how to make sure that she is checked and properly treated for allergies, sinusitis, and GERD, as well as describe how to eliminate and manage asthma triggers that stand as obstacles to her health and well-being.

3

An Asthma Diagnosis

What It Means . . . and What It Doesn't

IT SEEMS HARD to believe that only fifty years ago, children diagnosed with asthma were virtually shunned. Neither contagious nor invalids, they were removed from their homes and sheltered in asthma houses, away from parents, friends, and siblings. Similarly, asthma summer camps were designed to safeguard children with asthma from the rigors of exercise, sports, and swimming. The rationale at the time was to keep them away from environmental irritants, asthma triggers, house pets, and too much activity. The emphasis was to remove them from the asthma-triggering environment and from their parents. Rather than alter the environment and home life to support the health of the child, physicians performed a "parent-ectomy," believing it was important to get him away from parents, the irritants and allergens in the home, and the emotions of the family.

Although the goal of asthma housing and camps may have been to protect children, by today's standards, this approach seems isolating and stigmatizing. While we no longer adhere to a philosophy of segregating children with asthma, that philosophy was strong enough and lasted long enough to influence our beliefs and our responses to asthma today. Myths about the illness and about the children who develop it still exist. Often unspoken, they continue to have an impact on our thoughts, responses, and beliefs about asthma. It is important to be aware of the mythology of asthma and to be alert to the signs that you may be succumbing to a myth, outdated medical beliefs, and/or half-truths about your child's condition.

The Importance of a Healthy Perspective

As an asthma specialist who has delivered unwelcome news to thousands of parents, and as the grandparent of two children with asthma, I know that an asthma diagnosis can be extremely upsetting, even frightening. Despite the advances in treatment, it is still a chronic, incurable, and serious disease, and every parent has heard of at least one child who has struggled with asthma symptoms, been hospitalized, or was rushed to the emergency department.

I certainly can appreciate that parents need to give themselves the room to feel upset upon hearing that their child has asthma. My own response to learning that my granddaughter had asthma was anything but clinical. I felt quite sad and concerned, even though I knew she was in the hands of an excellent medical team and that her parents would be actively involved in working with her pediatrician to ensure that her asthma was controlled.

How a Diagnosis Can Affect You and Your Family

It is one thing to feel an initial panic or depression. However, it is quite another to sink into a depressed and hypervigilant state that wreaks havoc on the health and well-being of you and your family, which does nothing to help your child. Unfortunately, this reaction is extremely common. Parents will often respond to an asthma diagnosis with guilt or depression. They will silently wonder what they did wrong. If their child was originally misdiagnosed, they may blame themselves for not getting appropriate care sooner.

You may have begun reading this book with a sense that you had not done enough for your child or that you had allowed symptoms to continue for too long. Parents often feel guilty and angry with themselves and each other when they learn that the coughing or other symptoms were, in fact, asthma and not a viral infection, bad cold, or "just a cough." They return home in a cloud of confusion and fear, standing guard over their child's bedside, afraid to let him out to school or play and convinced that he is destined to be "sickly." Their constant worry and anxiety permeate and deal a serious blow to the quality of their family life. Research shows that a parent's emotional distress and anxiety, combined with a lack of social support for parents or the family, have a direct impact on asthma's influence on family life. In addition, relationships with siblings can be damaged, as other children come to resent the front-and-center role that asthma has in the family's life. They may feel neglected, as attention and concern are focused squarely on their asthmatic brother or sister, and they may act out, further heightening family tensions.

How It Affects Your Child

In turn, children with asthma cannot help but internalize the anxiety from parents, becoming worriers themselves. To make matters worse, this worrying and hypervigilance cultivate their passivity. They, too, become afraid to exercise or have fun, setting them up for a host of social and physical problems, including isolation and obesity. Children with asthma may resist the suffocating concern, or they may use it to gain more attention and compete with siblings for parental attention. In fact, some children may exaggerate symptoms that are actually improving, holding on to the special position of "sick child" within the family structure.

In addition to undermining emotional health and quality of life, all of this strain and anxiety can worsen asthma symptoms. We know that anxiety does not cause asthma, but it can make symptoms worse or precipitate an asthma episode. Some asthma specialists have dubbed the strong connection between the family's response to asthma and its ability to hinder asthma control "relationship inflammation."

Affecting Asthma Treatment and Management

Unremitting anxiety over his asthma can also get in the way of complying with medications and a treatment plan, and keep you from fully realizing the benefits of proactive asthma care. And, of course, it can have a dramatic and deleterious effect on you. Parenting is hard work in any case, and parenting a child with asthma presents added responsibilities and challenges. That is why the proactive asthma care approach, which you will first learn about in Chapter 6 of this book, will not only help your child, but will also benefit the entire family, giving you a sense of power and control in the face of a disease and a situation that can make parents feel helpless. You deserve the peace of mind and empowerment of this approach as much as does anyone else.

Debunking Common Myths About Asthma

If anxiety is a cornerstone of your daily life, if you find yourself worried that your child will die if he exercises, participates in active sports, dances, or plays the clarinet, that he will never grow or will be sickly, you may ask yourself why. Why are you plagued with these relentless concerns, even while you are learning that asthma is controllable and that children with asthma can live normal lives?

In my view, the new understanding of childhood asthma and the impact of the "asthma revolution" are no match for the deep-seated myths and stereotypes that are rooted in our psyche. These half-truths are kept alive through popular culture, misinformed teachers and coaches, and others who work with children—particularly in sports settings—and even, unfortunately, the medical profession. Conversely, there is also a set of what I call "minimizing myths"—the types that go to the other extreme and downplay childhood asthma. I have always believed that these minimizing myths were simply the other side of the anxiety coin, with parents trying to manage their fears by shrugging off asthma's seriousness. But, whether they paint a bleak or rosy picture, myths are powerful, either feeding anxiety or blinding you to asthma's realities. As a parent, you may be vulnerable to them.

Fears and Minimizing Myths About Asthma

Here is a rundown of some of the most pervasive and damaging myths that live on, despite all that we know:

• **A child with asthma is sickly—he can't be too active.** This is one of the most pernicious asthma myths, and the one that has stood the test of time. It is typically the first worry of parents and children and it is a hard myth to fight. Often, even when I tell parents that children not only can, but should, stay active and participate in sports, dance lessons, and gymnastics, the parents have a hard time believing me. The truth is that there are virtually no activities that an asthmatic child should not consider, provided that his asthma is well controlled. Some of our most accomplished athletes have reached the top of their game with asthma, including track star Jackie Joyner-Kersee, basketball players Isiah Thomas and Dominique Wilkins, Pittsburgh Steelers fullback Jerome Bettis, and Olympic swimmer Greg Louganis. Children with asthma can live normal, active lives, with only minor modifications (such as taking a puff from an inhaler before vigorous activity) along the way, if necessary.

- **There is a risk my child will die from asthma.** This terrifying myth is what keeps some parents awake at night or virtually glued to their child's bedside. While it is true that asthma is life-threatening, deaths from asthma are very rare, particularly in children. This is not to minimize the impact of learning that he has a chronic and serious disease. It is news that no parent wants to hear. But constant worry and stress about something that is so unlikely to occur make it impossible for you to take the positive and proactive steps you need to take to maintain control of his asthma and help raise him to be a proactive patient. You can't be empowered if you're feeling overwrought and over the edge.

- **The way to deal with asthma is not to dramatize it.** Asthma is a serious disease, and our ability to control its symptoms does not mean we can cure it. The truth is, asthma is chronic, and the inflammation of the airways is always present, even without symptoms. That is why it is so important to take daily medication to reduce inflammation, and not simply treat symptoms with an inhaler and avoid triggers.

- **Asthma is caused by stress and high emotions.** Asthma is a lung disease caused by airway inflammation and bronchoconstriction, but this old chestnut remains. It is true that an emotional episode, such as laughing, crying, or yelling can bring on asthma symptoms, but asthma is not caused by emotions. However, emotions do have an impact on asthma. There is research to show that anxiety, particularly anxiety from parents, causes children to feel anxious, too, and such stress and anxiety can prompt asthma symptoms. Breathing and relaxation exercises or psychotherapy may help your child relax and cope with asthma and may reduce anxiety; but they will have no influence on the airway inflammation that causes the disease.

• **Children outgrow asthma.** Unfortunately, asthma is chronic. In some people symptoms may ease as they get older, but the disease does not disappear. Fifty percent of all children with asthma either continue to have symptoms throughout their lives or see a return of symptoms in late adolescence and adulthood after a brief lull. The course of asthma is highly unpredictable, and physicians at this point cannot identify which children will see a lessening of symptoms as they grow older and which will not. However, some data suggest that children with more severe asthma, those who developed the disease very early in life, or those who have significant allergies along with asthma can expect lifelong symptoms.

Unwarranted Fears About Asthma Medications

In truth, asthma medicines, including inhaled steroids, are among the safest prescription drugs available to children. They do not cause the growth of extra hair or brain tumors or cause your child's growth to be permanently stunted. Those fears are most likely the result of many people confusing inhaled steroids for asthma with anabolic steroids, often abused by athletes. They are two entirely different compounds. And there is no difference in the height of adults who took asthma medication in childhood and those who did not. In fact, *untreated* asthma may inhibit growth.

Another unwarranted fear concerns the addictive nature of these medications. Asthma medications are not addictive and never have been. This myth may have grown out of the news stories concerning the addictive qualities of over-the-counter sprays for nasal congestion. Whatever its origins, this belief holds no validity. Often, parents think that taking a medicine every day implies that it is potentially addictive. But think about it: Do you feel the same way about cholesterol-lowering drugs that millions of adults take every day?

As with all medications, there are side effects, and not all asthma drugs are right for every child. That is why it is so important to watch for side effects, involve him in assessing how he is feeling after taking medications, and work with your health care professional to change the treatment plan, if necessary. (I will cover asthma medications and these fears in more detail in Chapter 4.)

Confronting Your Fears About Asthma

As a parent, you need to come to terms, in your own way, with the knowledge that your child has asthma. With the help of this book, I trust you will gain greater insight into why you may harbor unfounded fears and the damage that they can do to you, your asthmatic child, and your family. In tackling your fears, learning more about the antiquated understandings and notions of asthma that continue to exist even to this day, and separating fact from fiction, you can gain greater control over your anxiety and the ability to separate your emotional responses from the facts.

Learning more about asthma—what it is and what it isn't, working with your physician proactively (the main tenet of proactive asthma care), and teaching your child proactive asthma care will also help cultivate a sense of control that is often at the root of anxiety and stress. You might also find it helpful to join a support group in your community (your physician or nurse may know of some). The Allergy and Asthma Network Mothers of Asthmatics (www.aanma.org), the American Lung Association (www.lungusa.org), and the Asthma and Allergy Foundation of America (www.aafa.org) also run support groups through local chapters throughout the country.

The combination of self-awareness, knowledge, and support can provide an essential foundation for moving forward and putting an empowered outlook into practice. With knowledge and insight, you not only will help redefine asthma for yourself and your child, but can also be an asthma "myth buster" for other parents facing similar challenges.

4

Figuring Out the Medication Morass

IN ONE QUICK minute, you learn that your child has asthma. Then you are handed a prescription—many times, more than one—for asthma medications. In the blink of an eye, you are hurriedly told what the medications are, given an overview of how to use an inhaler or nebulizer, and ushered out of the office. In a blur, you pay your bill, take the trip to the pharmacy, and return home, hoping you will get it all straight as the weeks go on. Unfortunately, many parents and children don't get it all straight, through no fault of their own.

Asthma medications, taken consistently and correctly, are critical components of achieving a symptom-free life. Your child's asthma may have been developing for years without treatment, and the first few weeks require an aggressive approach to stop any further damage to the airways and get symptoms under control. Since asthma is a chronic disease of both inflammation *and* airway constriction, both need to be addressed with the appropriate medical treatment. Even when symptoms are mild or she feels fine, the inflammation and airway hypersensitivity are always present. This condition requires ongoing treatment if you want to avoid the emergency department visits and unscheduled trips to your physician's office that often result when asthma medications are not being taken as directed or when parents are unsure of how and when to administer them.

But many parents and children are never given enough guidance to ensure that they are using the devices properly. In truth, some physicians and health care professionals may not know how to use asthma devices themselves. Even if they do know how to use the devices properly, they fail to convey the information to parents and children. In addition, parents may forget dosages or make decisions to reduce the amount of medications prescribed without first consulting a health care professional. As a result, children don't get enough of the medication they need to reverse the course of their asthma.

The Challenges of Treatment

Coming to terms with the complexity of asthma treatment, particularly in the initial weeks following a diagnosis, is challenging. Asthma, as we know, is neither easy to understand nor simple to treat. The need for children with asthma to take several medications every day is further complicated by their need to learn *how* to take them. Most medications for childhood asthma need to be inhaled daily, and ensuring that your child has mastered proper inhalation techniques can be tricky.

Assuming you were given prescriptions for medications that will most help your child, you may not have been told what they were designed to do, when and how best to administer them, and what to do if she is having difficulty using an inhalation device (or is being uncooperative). For example, you may have been given a prescription for an inhaler to help draw medication into her lungs, but neither you nor she may have been trained on how to properly use the device. Even if your physician or nurse offered a quick run-through of how the inhaler works, you may not have mastered it, and your child may not be getting all of the medication she needs to improve. Furthermore, you and your child may not have been told just how important the medications are to her health and that compliance with the medication plan is critical.

What Is Your Child Taking?

The medicines and devices now available to treat asthma are impressive. As a physician, I have more at my disposal to help children with asthma than ever before. Moreover, the drugs for asthma are safer and more effective than in years past, and side effects are minimal. Yet the gap is still enormous between the advances in asthma and the standard treatment that most children receive.

Despite years of research underscoring the importance of treating asthma as a disease of inflammation with drugs that reduce or reverse the inflammation of the airways, many children continue to receive prescriptions that only manage the constriction of the airways. This undertreatment is only one of the issues that contribute to the medication morass. The mythology of asthma often gets in the way of sound treatment, too, with parents believing that too much medication will hurt their child. It is extremely common for parents to reduce the dosage of asthma medication on their own in an attempt to allay their own concerns that asthma medication may be harmful in some way.

To be sure, news reports of side effects associated with prescription drugs can be a cause for worry. I suspect that the concern surrounding asthma drugs derives from parents' fears about the use of steroids. Even if you have been giving her the recommended dose of inhaled corticosteroid, you may harbor fears that these drugs could harm your child. The fear of taking daily inhaled corticosteroids has been dubbed "steroid phobia" by physicians, and it is a serious issue. Research has shown that the fear of steroids may contribute to the fact that less than half of all patients with asthma take their inhaled corticosteroid medication as prescribed. Certainly, news reports of athletes abusing steroids have contributed to these fears, but I also believe that the medical community has not done a particularly good job of explaining the difference between harmful steroids and those that help.

There is an enormous difference between anabolic steroids and the inhaled corticosteroids used in asthma. *Anabolic steroids* are synthetic forms of the male sex hormone, testosterone; they are sometimes abused by athletes to build strength and endurance and can cause serious side effects. *Corticosteroids* are derived from completely different compounds. They are two entirely different drugs.

That said, your goal is to have your child's symptoms controlled with the fewest medications at the lowest doses possible. At the start of treatment, she will typically require the most medication to get symptoms under control. After a month or so, you should see significant improvement in symptoms, and she should be well on her way to a symptom-free life. Over time, you should also see a decrease in the amount of medication she needs to control her symptoms. Your physician should be as committed as you are to reducing the amount of medication she needs over time.

Medication and Education: *Why They Are So Crucial*

A good treatment plan requires the right kind of medication *and* education. The prescriptions are not enough. Equally important are knowing how and when to give the medication, feeling comfortable with medications and their safety, being made aware of their potential side effects, and being confident when using asthma devices. Your child, too, must be actively involved in learning about her medication, knowing when and how she should take it, how to use devices, and when to tell you if she is not feeling well after taking it.

But, as you may also have noticed from that first day in the physician's office, a comprehensive explanation of your child's medication, the purpose for each one, and how to administer—along with the critically important in-office training in how to use devices—may not have been part of the office visit or may have been too hurried. If you had questions, or if you understandably needed to ask the same one more than once, you may not have been given an answer that you fully understood. This is not a "patient problem" at all. Asthma and its treatment are complicated, so you, as a parent, and your child, the patient, deserve to take as much time as you need to understand the medication regimen. However, in most physician offices throughout the country, the necessary time and expertise may not be available.

As you've learned in previous chapters, parents—and children if they are old enough—need to supplement the information they receive from their health care professional to help fill in the gaps. This chapter is designed to do just that by providing:

- An overview of asthma medications, how they work, and their purposes and goals
- A description of the devices that you need to have and use properly to make sure that your child is getting enough medication to improve
- Responses to some common concerns that you may have regarding side effects

Becoming well versed in your child's asthma medication regimen is well worth the effort. When the right asthma medications are taken correctly, they pave the way to a life free of serious asthma episodes and symptoms while reducing and reversing the inflammation that is at the root of the symptoms.

The Long and Short of Asthma Medicines

Asthma medications are divided into two classes, each designed to address the two basic realities of asthma: that effective management requires treatment for constriction *and* inflammation of the airways. *Long-term control medications* are taken daily and over a long period of time to reduce airway inflammation and prevent inflammation from occurring, while maintaining control over symptoms and preventing serious asthma episodes. *Short-term, quick-relief medications* (also known as *rescue medications*) treat symptoms (such as coughing, wheezing, difficulty breathing, and chest tightness) and also prevent bronchospasm resulting from exercise.

It is not uncommon for children to receive a prescription for a short-term medication only, but it is insufficient to achieving symptom-free asthma goals. Short-term medications do nothing to reduce or prevent the inflammation that produces the hypersensitivity and bronchospasm in the first place.

The first step in gaining the confidence to assess whether her treatment plan is adequate is to know what medications exist, which ones are most often used to treat children with asthma, and which ones your child may be taking. What follows is an overview of short- and long-term medications, what they do, their benefits, and their limitations. I will include the generic names for the drugs, as well as the brand names.

Long-Term Control Medications

The medications described in this section and listed in Table 4.1 are taken daily on a long-term basis. To reduce the frequency and the severity of asthma symptoms, your child needs to take a long-term control medication even when she is feeling fine.

Table 4.1 Long-Term Control Medications Available in the United States for Children

Generic (Brand) Name	Type of Medication	How Used	Possible Side Effects/Drawbacks
Cromolyn sodium (Intal)	Mast cell stabilizer	Inhaled	Safety is the primary advantage, but a 4- to 6-week trial may be necessary to see any effect. Typical dose with an inhaler may be inadequate to effectively treat symptoms; use with a nebulizer may be best for some children.
Nedocromil sodium (Tilade)	Mast cell stablizer	Inhaled	Unpleasant taste
Beclomethasone HFA (Qvar)	Corticosteroid	Inhaled	Cough, hoarseness, thrush
Budesonide (Pulmicort)	Corticosteroid	Inhaled	Cough, hoarseness, thrush
Fluticasone (Flovent)	Corticosteroid	Inhaled	Cough, hoarseness, thrush
Mometasone (Asmanex)	Corticosteroid	Inhaled	Cough, hoarseness, thrush
Flunisolide (Aerobid)	Corticosteroid	Inhaled	Cough, hoarseness, thrush
Triamcinolone (Azmacort)	Corticosteroid	Inhaled	Cough, hoarseness, thrush
Formoterol (Foradil)	Long-acting beta-2 agonist	Inhaled	Increased heart rate, tremor, insomnia
Salmeterol (Serevent Diskus)	Long-acting beta-2 agonist	Inhaled	Increased heart rate, tremor, insomnia
Fluticasone/salmeterol (Advair)	Combined medication (corticosteroid and long-acting beta-2 agonist)	Inhaled	Increased heart rate, tremor, insomnia
Montelukast (Singulair)	Leukotriene modifier	Orally	Few side effects
Zafirlukast (Accolate)	Leukotriene modifier	Orally	Few side effects

Theophylline		Orally	
Methylprednisolone* (Medrol)	Corticosteroid	Orally	Increased heart rate, tremor, nausea, vomiting, headache This type of drug has side effects if taken long term, so should be used in short courses or "bursts" to establish control when beginning asthma treatment or during a period when symptoms worsen. Short-term treatment should continue until symptoms improve, usually within 3 to 10 days.
Prednisolone* (Prelone, Pediapred, Orapred)	Corticosteroid	Orally	See Methylprednisolone
Prednisone* (Deltasone, Prednisone Intensol)	Corticosteroid	Orally	See Methylprednisolone
Omalizumab (Xolair)	Anti-IgE antibody	Injection	Few side effects, but to be used only in children over age 12; injections every 2 to 4 weeks in physician's office

*Rarely used long term in children.

Cromolyn Sodium (Intal) and Nedocromil Sodium (Tilade)

Both of these medications are inhaled, and they improve symptoms by reducing inflammation and improving lung function. They can be used to prevent asthma symptoms due to certain triggers—such as exposure to cold air, exercise, or allergens—by taking the medication prior to exposure. When taken regularly, they decrease overreaction of the airways, which helps control asthma and decreases the need for quick-relief medication. They are known to be quite safe but are much less effective anti-inflammatory medication than the newer long-acting drugs—the inhaled corticosteroids. Because they are less effective, they are rarely prescribed.

Inhaled Corticosteroids

These are the most effective long-term medications we have to control the symptoms and inflammation of asthma. They help regardless of how severe the asthma may be, and when taken daily, they significantly reduce the need for short-acting rescue medications. Studies consistently demonstrate that even low doses help and make a significant difference in children's lives. Compared with some types of short-acting treatments, inhaled corticosteroids significantly reduce serious asthma episodes. They are also more effective than certain long-acting medications, reducing asthma episodes by up to 45 percent over other treatments. Unfortunately, many children do not receive a prescription for an inhaled corticosteroid or may fail to take their medication daily to prevent symptoms.

Six inhaled corticosteroids are currently available in the United States, including fluticasone propionate (Flovent HFA), triamcinolone (Azmacort), budesonide (Pulmicort), beclomethasone HFA (Qvar), mometasone (Asmanex), and flunisolide (Aerobid). Inhaled corticosteroids are considered a cornerstone of asthma treatment, but many children do not receive a prescription or may fail to take their medication as needed. Studies have shown that the majority of children hospitalized for asthma are there because they failed to take their inhaled corticosteroids. This is unfortunate, since we know that early use of these drugs in even the youngest children and infants can have a positive impact on their asthma over time.

The reasons why children often do not get the amount of inhaled corticosteroid they need are complex. To be sure, taking these medicines requires skill on the part of parents and older children. They are given to young children through an inhaler or through a nebulizer (a complete discussion of asthma devices follows), and learning how to use an inhaler and nebulizer takes time and patience.

As a parent, you may also have heard of the side effects of these drugs—notably the possibility that children's growth will be stunted—and may avoid them. There has been a great deal of research in the area of children's growth and use of inhaled corticosteroids, and the most recent findings, based on large clinical trials that tracked children's growth, found that any effect on growth was minimal and reversible. In other words, low to medium doses of inhaled corticosteroids may have the potential to lower the rate of growth in the first year of treatment (amounting to an average of less than one-half an inch of height), but that difference in the rate of growth narrows as the years go on. In fact, long-term growth studies, which tracked the heights of children for a number of years, found that when they reached adulthood, those treated with inhaled corticosteroids in childhood were no shorter than their non-asthmatic peers or siblings. Studies have also put to rest fears that these drugs have a negative effect on the density of children's bones. After monitoring bone density in children, studies found that there was no decrease in bone mineral density.

While the research shows that inhaled corticosteroids are highly effective and safe, it is important that your child receive the lowest dose possible to achieve the desired result, and that your physician monitor her growth to be sure that any impact is minimal. There may be extremely rare cases when growth is significantly hindered, and while any problems are unlikely, it is prudent to check.

Proper inhalation techniques are equally important. We know that these drugs are safe when given in low to moderate doses. Taking in too much could have a negative impact and produce other side effects. It is also important to rinse the mouth thoroughly after inhalation, as these drugs have been known to cause *oral candidiasis* (thrush) and hoarseness if they linger in the mouth and throat for too long. Also, it is best not to swallow these drugs, as they can be absorbed through the gastrointestinal tract.

Table 4.2 gives you an overview of the typical doses of some inhaled corticosteroids for children. Using this chart, you can check where your child falls and discuss the dose with her physician if you have any concerns.

Leukotriene Modifiers

These drugs are tablets—montelukast (Singulair) and zafirlukast (Accolate)—that put the brakes on the activity of *leukotrienes*, powerful biochemicals that promote the work of inflammatory cells (especially eosinophils), increase production of mucus and airway swelling, and cause bronchoconstriction. If your child has only mild persistent asthma, Singulair can be used alone. In cases of moderate asthma or in asthma patients who also have allergic rhinitis, some physicians prescribe these drugs along with inhaled corticosteroids to accelerate

Table 4.2 Comparative Daily Dosages for Inhaled Corticosteroids (in Children)

Drug	Low Daily Dose	Medium Daily Dose	High Daily Dose
Beclomethasone HFA (40 or 80 mcg/puff)	80–160 mcg	160–320 mcg	More than 320 mcg
Budesonide DPI (200 mcg/inhalation)	200–400 mcg	400–800 mcg	More than 800 mcg
With a nebulizer	0.5 mg	1.0 mg	2.0 mg
Flunisolide (250 mcg/puff)	500–750 mcg	1,000–1,250 mcg	More than 1,250 mcg
Fluticasone (MDI: 44, 110, or 220 mcg/puff)	88–176 mcg	176–440 mcg	More than 440 mcg
Triamcinolone acetonide (100 mcg/puff)	400–800 mcg	800–1,200 mcg	More than 1,200 mcg
Mometasone (200 mcg/puff)	200 mcg	200–400 mcg	More than 400 mcg

Source: U.S. Department of Health and Human Services; National Institutes of Health; National Heart, Lung, and Blood Institute

symptom improvement. Singulair can also protect a child against asthma symptoms brought on by exercise.

Long-Acting Beta-2 Agonists

These drugs, which include formoterol (Foradil) and salmeterol (Serevent), are add-ons to treatment with inhaled corticosteroids and should never be prescribed alone, since they do not treat airway inflammation. Recent studies have shown that they could actually prompt a serious asthma episode if used regularly without inhaled corticosteroids. They work by relaxing the bronchial muscles and are especially helpful in children who have asthma symptoms at night. They are also effective in preventing asthma symptoms brought on by exercise. Your physician may also consider them to improve symptom control without increasing the dose of inhaled corticosteroid. These drugs are inhaled and keep working for about twelve hours. They are taken once or twice daily, depending on her need.

Theophylline

This is one of the oldest asthma drugs and is used less and less in treatment, due to its side effects. Like the leukotriene modifiers and long-acting beta-2 agonists, it should be considered an add-on to inhaled corticosteroids to help control symptoms. Taken in tablet form, it works by opening up the airways. Its side effects are considerable, and your physician must monitor dosage and levels of the drug in your child's blood very closely. Even low doses of theophylline have been known to cause nausea, nervousness, headache, and insomnia. In some cases, the drug can lead to vomiting, irregular heartbeat, tremor, shakiness, and, rarely, convulsions. For example, if your child needs to be treated for a bacterial infection, certain medications—including some antibiotics—can cause blood levels of theophylline to rise, thereby increasing its risk for side effects.

Anti-IgE Antibody

Known as omalizumab (Xolair), this medication binds to IgE in the circulation and blocks its attachment to the surface of mast cells and basophils, preventing them from responding to allergens. It needs to be injected in the physician's office every two to four weeks and can be given only to children age twelve and older. If your child has moderate to severe allergic asthma and has had hospitalizations despite ongoing treatment with inhaled corticosteroids, then you may want to discuss adding Xolair to her regimen.

Xolair is known to reduce the rate of serious asthma episodes and the need for unscheduled physician visits, emergency department treatment, and hospitalizations.

Short-Acting, Quick-Relief Medications

Short-acting medications, also known as rescue medications and viewed in Table 4.3, will help your child during an asthma episode. You may find that currently she needs to use quick-relief medications several times a week, but it is the goal of proactive asthma care and this book, to truly limit the need for these medications over time with the proper use of long-term treatment and effective management strategies. The ongoing need for these drugs should be a red flag for any parent, since a child's dependence on them is a direct measure of poor asthma management. However, in the short term, she may need them. Over time, as symptoms improve, she should need them only to prevent asthma symptoms before exercise, if at all.

Table 4.3 Quick-Relief Asthma Medications Available in the United States for Children

Generic (Brand) Name	Type of Medication	How Used	Possible Side Effects/Drawbacks
Albuterol	Short-acting beta-2 agonist	Inhaled	Tremor, increased heart rate
Proventil	Short-acting beta-2 agonist	Inhaled	Tremor, increased heart rate
Ventolin	Short-acting beta-2 agonist	Inhaled	Tremor, increased heart rate
Xopenex	Short-acting beta-2 agonist	Inhaled	Tremor, increased heart rate
Maxair	Short-acting beta-2 agonist	Inhaled	Tremor, increased heart rate
Alupent	Short-acting beta-2 agonist	Inhaled	Tremor, increased heart rate
Atrovent	Anticholinergic	Inhaled	Dry mouth

Short-Acting Beta-2 Agonists

These drugs are synonymous with asthma medication and are what most people first think of when they think of asthma treatment. Albuterol, Ventolin, Proventil, Maxair, Xopenex, and Alupent are among the first prescriptions you may have received for your child's asthma. While these medications do provide effective treatment for asthma symptoms—coughing, wheezing, shortness of breath, rapid breathing, and chest tightness—and for preventing symptoms when taken right before exercise, their effectiveness is short-lived.

Over-the-counter versions (Primatene Mist, Bronk-Aid) are ineffective, have numerous side effects, and have been linked to asthma-related deaths. *They should be avoided.*

Studies have suggested that using short-acting beta-2 agonist medications for months may lead to tolerance to the drugs' effects and possibly poor disease control. In addition, they do have side effects, including certain types of irregular heartbeat and palpitations, tremor, and a reduction in the body's supply of potassium. The goal of effective asthma treatment should include minimizing or eliminating use of these drugs. In no case should they be the only medication your child is using for asthma symptoms. If she needs to use them more than twice a week (except for prevention of exercise-induced asthma), then that is a sure sign that the asthma is not being properly managed with inhaled corticosteroids and other long-term medications. In other words, your child is only being treated halfway. Through the proactive asthma care approach, you will learn in subsequent chapters how to correct this situation with your physician.

Oral Corticosteroids

These medications should be considered as stopgap measures, at best. You may receive a prescription for prednisone or branded prednisolone formulations (including Medrol, Prelone, Orapred, and Pediapred) if she is having serious asthma symptoms that are not helped with a rescue medication. You and your physician may want to consider a short course (usually three to five days) of oral corticosteroids to quickly decrease serious symptoms and prevent a relapse.

However, unlike inhaled corticosteroids, these drugs do have some significant side effects, especially when used for months at a time.

Among them are glucose intolerance, weight gain, increased blood pressure, osteoporosis, cataracts, suppressed immune system, mood disorders (including psychosis), and decreased growth. Electing to use these drugs is a serious decision, and the benefits need to outweigh the risks. If your child is on an oral corticosteroid longer than a few weeks, her use of the medicine must be tapered off over a period of time (depending on how long she has been taking it). She should then be switched to a safer inhaled corticosteroid at an appropriate dose for long-term management. In my practice, I do not have any child with chronic asthma on oral corticosteroids.

Anticholinergics

Medications such as ipratropium bromide (Atrovent)—an inhaled bronchodilator—are occasionally prescribed in addition to inhaled corticosteroids. At times, these drugs are prescribed along with albuterol or are reserved for children who cannot tolerate albuterol. They do have the occasional unpleasant side effect, such as dry mouth and sore throat.

Asthma Devices: The Best Route to Symptom Relief

Inhalation is the preferred route of delivery for most asthma drugs. It delivers the drug more effectively to your child's airways, reduces the possibility of side effects, and relieves symptoms faster. But the best route is not always the easiest traveled. Giving any medication to a child can be challenging, but those that are inhaled require skill and coordination. Since most asthma medications need to be inhaled each day—even if your child feels fine—and since they are pivotal to her improvement, it is important that you, as a parent, are confident that she is using the inhalation device correctly and that the right amount of drug is getting into her lower airways.

Types of Devices

There are three types of inhalation devices: a metered-dose inhaler, a nebulizer, and a dry-powder inhaler. A *metered-dose inhaler* (MDI) is a pressurized container that uses a chemical propellant to push the medication through the inhaler. [The chlorofluorocarbon, or CFC, propellants that had been used in MDIs are being phased out of use for environmental reasons. As of 2008, all CFCs will be replaced by a different propellant, hydrofluoroalkanes (HFAs), as per a U.S. Food and Drug Administration ruling. At present, some MDIs have HFA propellants.] With most MDIs, the user draws the medication into the airways by breathing slowly in long, deep breaths. *Dry-powder inhalers* deliver medication without using a propellant. Dry-powder inhalers and breath-activated devices require *rapid*, deep breaths in. A *nebulizer* (a small air compressor connected to a generator) delivers a fine liquid mist of medication through a tube or mask that fits over the nose and mouth.

Coordinating breaths through an inhaler can be downright difficult for adults, not to mention children. Your child may find it much easier to use an inhaler along with a *spacer* (also called a *holding chamber*), which is attached to a soft mask and helps deliver a greater amount of medication directly into the lower airways, where it is intended to go, rather than into the throat. Over the age of five, however, most children can use a spacer without a mask.

Spacers fit on the end of the inhaler. If your child has trouble with the metered-dose inhaler, *breath-activated devices* or a dry-powder inhaler may be a better option, as many children find that these feel more natural and less forced than using an MDI. Spacers are not needed for dry-powder devices.

If your child simply cannot or will not use an inhaler, or if you have a baby or toddler (under the age of five), then a nebulizer would be your best option. Nebulizers are particularly efficient in administering short-acting beta-2 agonists and inhaled corticosteroids. Though using one can be time-consuming, with proper instruction and the encouragement of your physician, you should find your comfort level quickly. It should be used with a properly fitting mask in babies and very young children and with a mouthpiece in children over five. It should never be used by blowing it by the child's face or when a child is crying. (When your child cries, the medicine is not inhaled properly and is not distributed evenly through the airways.)

All three devices, particularly the metered-dose inhaler, require careful, step-by-step training from your physician or other health care professional before you leave the physician's office. If you already have a device but are concerned that you or your child may not be using it correctly, take it back to the physician's office and ask for a demonstration. In fact, you should bring your devices to every office visit and ask for retraining on a routine basis.

A Step-by-Step Guide to Using the Asthma Devices Correctly

The following step-by-step guidelines are adapted from the American Academy of Allergy, Asthma and Immunology's 2003 publication "Pediatric Asthma: Promoting Best Practice." You can follow it here to check whether you are using asthma devices correctly.

How to Use a Metered-Dose Inhaler

The following steps are for one puff! If your child's physician recommends additional puffs, repeat the same steps. If your child will be using a spacer or holding chamber (which can make the process easier for many children), remove the caps from both the MDI and the spacer, and look inside to make sure there are no objects. Attach the MDI to the spacer, shake it well, and follow the steps for the MDI. Never put more than one puff in the spacer at one time.

In young children, the MDI is used with a spacer attached to a mask. The mask is applied tightly to your child's face. One puff of the medicine is released into the chamber, and she takes five to six breaths.

If you hear a whistle sound when your child inhales using a spacer, that means she is breathing too quickly. Ask her to inhale more slowly.

1. Remove the cap, and hold the inhaler upright.
2. Shake the inhaler.
3. Have your child tilt her head slightly backward and fully breathe out.
4. Put the mouthpiece in her mouth between her teeth. Make sure she closes her lips around it. Alternatively, many specialists recommend the "open mouth" technique (the inhaler is placed about an inch from her open mouth).

5. Press down on the inhaler to release the medicine, while she starts to breathe in slowly. (Your child should continue to breathe in slowly for at least 5 seconds, if possible.)
6. Take the inhaler out of her mouth while she holds her breath for about 10 seconds. (This allows the medicine to reach deep into the lungs.) Then have her breathe out. Wait approximately 30 seconds, and repeat according to your management plan.

How to Use a Breath-Activated Metered-Dose Inhaler

Again, this is one puff.

1. Remove the mouthpiece by pulling the cover lip down.
2. Inspect the mouthpiece for any objects.
3. Hold the device upright, with arrows pointing up, and push the lever up. (It should snap into place.)
4. Hold the device around the middle, and shake.
5. Ask your child to exhale.
6. Help her place the device in her mouth, closing her lips tightly around the mouthpiece.
7. Ask her to breathe in deeply through her mouth, and let her know she will hear a click when the medicine is released. (Tell her to keep inhaling.)
8. Remove the device, and have her hold her breath for 10 seconds.
9. Ask her to exhale.

How to Use a Nebulizer

1. Assemble the nebulizer according to the manufacturer's directions.
2. Put your child's medicine into the nebulizer cup.
3. Attach the mouthpiece or mask to the nebulizer.
4. Put the mouthpiece in your child's mouth, and make sure she closes her lips tightly around it. (If using a mask, consult with her physician or your pharmacist.)

5. Turn on the nebulizer.
6. She should take slow, deep breaths in through the mouth and should hold each breath for 1 to 2 seconds before breathing out.
7. Continue until all the medicine is gone from the cup, which typically takes about 10 minutes.

How to Use a Dry-Powder Inhaler

There are four different types of dry-powder inhalers, and you should carefully read the directions and work with your physician to learn how to use yours. The following is a general guide to using each type.

Diskus (Advair, Serevent)

1. Hold the diskus horizontally in one hand.
2. Put the thumb of your other hand on the thumb grip, and push away, as far as possible, until the mouthpiece appears and snaps into position.
3. With the same thumb, push the lever away from you until it clicks.
4. Tell your child to exhale.
5. Before she inhales, help her place the diskus mouthpiece in her mouth, closing her lips tightly around it.
6. Ask her to breathe through her mouth, as quickly and deeply as possible.
7. Ask her to hold her breath, while you count to 10.
8. Before she exhales, ask her to remove the diskus from her mouth.
9. Ask her to exhale.
10. Ask her to rinse her mouth with water and then spit it out, without swallowing. (Advair only.)

Turbuhaler (Pulmicort)

1. Twist the cover to the right, and lift it off.
2. Holding the device upright, with the mouthpiece facing upward, twist the colored grip to the right as far as it

will go. Then turn it to the left, as far as possible, until it clicks.

3. Tell your child to exhale.
4. Place the mouthpiece in her mouth and ask her to close her lips tightly around it.
5. Ask her to inhale through her mouth as quickly and deeply as possible.
6. Ask her to hold her breath while you count to 10, then exhale.
7. Ask her to rinse her mouth with water and then spit it out, without swallowing.

Twisthaler (Asmanex)

1. Hold the inhaler straight up with the pink portion (the base) on the bottom. The Twisthaler needs to be in the upright position when you take off the cap to make sure that your child gets the right amount of medicine with each dose.
2. Holding the pink base, twist the cap in a counterclockwise direction to remove it. As you lift off the cap, the dose counter on the base will count down by one until the last dose in the package. This action loads the device with the medicine.
3. Have your child exhale fully, and then bring the Twisthaler to her mouth with the mouthpiece facing toward her. Place it in her mouth, holding it in a horizontal position. Have her firmly close her lips around the mouthpiece and take a fast, deep breath.
4. Remove the Twisthaler from her mouth and have her hold her breath for about 10 seconds, or as along as she comfortably can.
5. Ask her to rinse her mouth with water and then spit it out, without swallowing.
6. Wipe the mouthpiece dry and immediately replace the cap, closing it firmly. (When you hear a click, the cap is completely closed.) Make sure the arrow is in line with the dose-counter window, to ensure that the device is fully loaded for the next dose.

Aerolizer Inhaler (Foradil)

1. Pull one capsule from the blister pack by tearing along the slotted lines.
2. Take the capsule out of its package by peeling off the paper backing and pushing the capsule through the foil.
3. Following the direction of the arrow on the mouthpiece, twist the mouthpiece open.
4. Place the capsule in the chamber, and twist it closed.
5. Hold the inhaler upright, pressing both side buttons in. (This punctures the capsule and makes a clicking sound.)
6. Tell your child to exhale completely.
7. Turn the inhaler on its side (horizontally), making sure the blue bottoms are pointing to the sides.
8. Ask your child to tilt her head back slightly.
9. Have her place the mouthpiece in her mouth and close her lips tightly around it.
10. Ask her to take a deep, rapid breath. (If you don't hear a whirring sound, the capsule may be stuck, so tap the side of the inhaler to loosen the capsule, and ask her to inhale again.)
11. Ask her to remove the inhaler from her mouth and hold her breath while you count to 10, and then have her exhale.
12. Look inside the inhaler to make sure that all of the powder from the capsule was inhaled. (If not, then repeat the steps.)

Common Asthma Inhaler Mistakes

If it seems like there is a lot to think about and master when it comes to asthma devices, there is. That is why I tell my patients to ask for assistance—from physicians, the office nurse, or a pharmacist—until they are sure that they and their child have mastered it. However, there are some common mistakes that virtually everyone makes in the beginning, particularly if your child uses a metered-dose inhaler. Here is a list of what to watch out for and correct early on, so that your child can begin experiencing relief from symptoms as quickly as possible.

- Your child doesn't breathe out fully before pressing the inhaler.
- Your child doesn't breathe in through her mouth.
- Your child doesn't breathe evenly and deeply.
- Either you or your child doesn't press the inhaler right at the start of her inhaling.
- Your child doesn't continue to inhale while she is pressing down.
- You press more than once during each inhalation.
- Your child doesn't hold her breath for 10 seconds.

The Steps in Asthma Treatment

When asthma experts speak to their primary-care peers in the health care profession—pediatricians, family practice physicians, and other health care professionals—they encourage them to follow a series of steps in asthma treatment. Known as a stepwise approach, it holds to the belief that aggressive treatment, including use of a variety of medications, may be necessary to get asthma under control, but that medication should be "stepped down" when symptoms improve. Gaining control of asthma in the shortest time possible is the goal, and that may mean that your child is taking inhaled and oral corticosteroids, or more than two types of inhaled medications or pills, for a short period of time. Once the asthma is under control, however, the goal is to have her take the least amount of medication necessary.

Here are the steps, based on the severity of symptoms. Your child should receive enough medication and the right kinds of medication to eliminate symptoms at the outset. If her symptoms continue and she doesn't experience rapid improvement, then your physician should "step up" to the higher level, after making sure that your child is using the medication properly, is taking it as prescribed, and knows how to use her asthma device to get enough of the drug into her airways. Once symptoms have improved, you and your physician can discuss "stepping down" to the lower level of asthma medication.

The following sections describe the levels of asthma symptoms that physicians use to discuss the severity of a child's disease, and what medications and combinations they should use to effectively manage symptoms and get them under control.

For Severe Asthma Symptoms

If your child is experiencing symptoms continually or so frequently that they completely interfere with day-to-day activities, your physician may take the following steps to get them under control.

- Take high doses of inhaled corticosteroid along with a long-acting inhaled beta-2 agonist. (Children under age five do better with a nebulizer than with an inhaler.)
- If necessary, your child may need the addition of an oral corticosteroid in either tablet or liquid form, depending on her age. (Because of their side effects, your physician should make every effort to keep the dose of oral medication to no more than 60 milligrams per day and to take her off them as soon as possible—i.e., within 7 to 10 days.)

For Moderate Persistent Asthma

If your child has symptoms every day and more than one night a week, then she has "moderate persistent asthma," and your physician may take the following steps to get it under control.

- **If she is under age five:** Your child may take a medium to high dose of inhaled corticosteroid. In addition, some children age four and older may be able to use a long-acting beta-2 agonist, and those age two and above can use a leukotriene modifier as an alternative.
- **If she is over age five:** Treatment is similar, but your physician may start either with a medium to high dose of inhaled corticosteroid alone or with a low to medium dose of inhaled corticosteroid with a long-acting beta-2 agonist. He may increase the dose somewhat to achieve symptom control or add a leukotriene modifier.
- **Xolair might be considered as an add-on treatment.** This add-on is for children over age twelve. However, it should be considered if your child has severe asthma episodes and ends up in the hospital despite ongoing care, or if she has moderate to severe asthma that is

not under control, causing her to miss school and extracurricular activities or forcing her to take frequent courses of oral corticosteroids.

For Mild Persistent Asthma

If symptoms are not daily but occur more than twice a week and two nights per month, she has what physicians call "mild persistent asthma" and does require daily medication. Your physician should prescribe her the following medications:

- A low-dose inhaled corticosteroid
- As an alternative, a leukotriene modifier or cromolyn sodium

For Mild Intermittent Asthma

The only type of asthma that does not require daily medication is mild intermittent asthma. If your child has symptoms less than two days a week and no more than two nights a month, then she can get by on the occasional puff of short-acting beta-2 agonist medication to control mild symptoms (or before exercise). However, if she needs the inhaler more than twice a week, then she should be stepped up to "mild persistent" treatment. Frequent use of quick-acting medication is a signal that her asthma is not under control.

Children with mild intermittent asthma often go for long periods of normal lung function with no symptoms, only to experience severe episodes. At that point, the best treatment may be a course of oral corticosteroids to quickly eliminate the symptoms. If these severe episodes occur frequently (e.g., every six weeks), then she should be treated like a child with moderate persistent asthma.

Your physician—together with you and your child—should make the decision of how much and which type of medication(s) to prescribe according to your child's symptoms, their frequency, their severity, and her overall health history. Provided your health care professional has developed a sound asthma treatment plan, all medications are being taken as directed, and efforts have been made to minimize the asthma triggers found at home and at school, symptoms should decrease almost immediately, and your child should be on her way to achieving her asthma goals. Within three months or so, your health care professional should have begun discussing the possibility of reducing medications—in dose, frequency, or overall number. Reducing medications is the stepwise goal, but that can happen only if there is control of asthma symptoms.

If you don't feel that progress has been made, even by following the treatment plan, or if your child remains far too reliant on short-acting, quick-relief medications, then Part II of this book is aimed at turning around those and other stubborn situations. Proactive asthma care is the name I give to my simple but effective approach to dealing with your physician and other health care professionals, and using the information you now have about your child's disease to make sure you get the best help possible. Far from creating an adversarial climate with your health care professional, it will foster a true partnership, improve the quality of your child's office visits, and ultimately, give her the promise of a symptom-free life and an empowered future of her own.

5

What About Alternatives?

The Pros and the Cons of
Natural Treatments

AS THE PARENT of any child with asthma knows, life can be challenging. Parents and their children must take on an enormous responsibility to learn about and manage an extremely complicated chronic condition. It is difficult enough to increase your asthma IQ and that of your child, learn how to use asthma devices, become familiar with the peak-flow meter and how to use it to monitor your child's breathing, and work with schools and day-care personnel to extend the environmental controls you have put in place into your child's other environments.

Asthma also demands a certain vigilance and determination from you and other family members and caregivers. A certain degree of spontaneity is lost as a child with asthma needs to plan and anticipate possible asthma-inducing scenarios. Childhood asthma is sobering for parent and child.

In my busy California practice, my colleagues and I base our asthma treatments on strategies backed by years and years of research and clinical study. My four-week plan for symptom relief (covered in the chapters in Part II) is grounded in scientific data and evidence. The stepwise approach, the red-green-yellow symptom management tool, the use of asthma diaries, and the emphasis on environmental controls at home, school, and day care are backed by years of experience with thousands of patients and their families. So, too, is my use of pharmaceutical drugs to treat and prevent asthma symptoms in children, which has been studied extensively in well-controlled clinical trials. The side effects, such as jitteriness, are annoying and unpleasant but infrequent. The serious concerns of corticosteroids and their relationship to a reduction in growth have been addressed, and we find that there are no lasting effects. Children may have a temporary slowdown in growth that may be imperceptible, but the rate of growth resumes at a normal clip within a year or so.

Factors Other than Medication That Can Affect Treatment

Pharmaceutical drugs are only one aspect of asthma treatment. Environmental controls and immunotherapy—two nondrug approaches—are crucial and need to be applied by parents and physicians to eliminate symptoms. No amount of treatment with any asthma or allergy medication will help a child whose parents insist on smoking or who keep a cat in the house if the child has cat allergy.

How Parents Unknowingly Contribute to the Problem

Even when children use their inhaler each day and monitor their airway with a peak-flow meter, parents may still find that they haven't conscientiously attended to the nondrug aspects of asthma care. They may smoke outside the home, failing to recognize that even smoke on their clothing can trigger an asthma episode in their child. Cigarette by-products have been detected in urine tests of children living with parents who limit their cigarette smoking to outside the home, which strongly suggests that any contact with smoke or materials that have been in contact with smoke can spark asthma symptoms. They may have difficulty keeping the family cat out of their child's room but then fail to come to terms with the fact that the cat needs to go. They may make the necessary adjustments at home, but then not take action with schools, day-care centers, and camps to make sure that their child is safeguarded when she leaves the house.

How Physicians Unknowingly Affect Treatment

Time-stretched family physicians and pediatricians may unwittingly add to the problem. They may miss some of the more subtle clues that suggest that other factors—sinusitis, food allergy, and gastroesophageal reflux disease—may underlie asthma symptoms. For example, no amount of pharmaceutical intervention can help a child who has not been properly diagnosed with an allergy to milk products. In addition, some physicians may overrely on quick-relief medications (which have a number of side effects) without incorporating anti-inflammatory corticosteroid medication into the asthma management plan. In their interactions with parents, they may jump quickly over environmental controls and allergy testing, which are critical to reducing not only symptoms but also the need for high and frequent doses of asthma drugs.

As I've discussed previously, some physicians may find it difficult to carve out the time needed to educate parents and children on the full spectrum of environmental control issues, leaving everyone unclear, confused, or uninformed about the myriad of factors that can prompt asthma episodes in children. They may overlook the strong role that allergies play in childhood asthma, as well as the need for allergy testing and immunotherapy.

Alternatives and Your Child

The time-tested, established nondrug treatment of controlling your child's environment—from quitting smoking to using HEPA filters to finding a new home for the family pet—can reduce symptoms practically overnight. They are difficult to achieve and may require a financial investment in filters, new bedding, pillow covers, and even redecorating a child's room, replacing carpets and upholstered furniture, but they are a critical adjunct to pharmacologic treatment. Allergy immunotherapy—the somewhat inconvenient, uncomfortable shots—

also is an important nondrug treatment that is highly effective and safe, basically curing allergies and often eliminating or sharply reducing the need for antihistamines and other allergy medications.

In short, environmental controls and immunotherapy to treat and eliminate respiratory allergies, as the safe and effective nondrug asthma treatments, need to have equal time with asthma drugs in the management of asthma in children. They pose a challenge for parents, families, and even physicians, but they are essential, and as we've seen, form the cornerstone of the four-week program—in essence, a large part of what makes the program "proactive." Parents and children need to take action and implement changes throughout their lives to get rid of asthma symptoms. This proactive stance is also the posture you as a parent need to take to reduce the number and doses of drugs in treating your child's asthma—a strong desire for most parents and children.

Combined, the three cornerstones of asthma treatment—environmental controls, immunotherapy, and asthma drugs—eliminate symptoms and reduce your child's reliance on medication over time. The freedom of having to take as few drugs as possible and the lifting of restrictions on activities are what restore a true quality of life to your child and your family. Simply put, the right asthma management changes your lives.

Why Some Parents Are Reluctant About Medication

Some parents are reluctant to have their child take any drugs at all. It is not an uncommon experience in my practice. We've taken a history, administered the spirometry, and established an asthma diagnosis. We've discussed a treatment plan and reviewed use of asthma inhalers and other devices. It's at that point that some parents will share their concerns about any kind of drug therapy. They worry about side effects and don't like the idea of putting foreign substances in their child's body. As I discussed in Chapter 4, occasionally they confuse corticosteroids with the steroids that make headlines when athletes abuse those drugs (which are a completely different substance altogether). I can sympathize.

There have been numerous problems with pharmaceutical drugs, and some problems have resulted in products being pulled from the market. The headlines concerning Vioxx, often prescribed to treat arthritis, and the rare but dangerous side effects from certain anticholesterol medications (Baycol, a statin to treat high cholesterol, was taken from the market because of severe side effects) are troubling and understandably prompt parents to call into question the mechanisms by which all drugs are approved and regulated. The news stories concerning steroids almost never discuss that they are a form of the male sex hormone testosterone and not the therapeutic corticosteroids prescribed for asthma and other diseases. Not all pharmaceutical drugs are created equal, and those indicated for the treatment of childhood asthma have been used for years and are proven safe and effective—not only because they have been approved by the Food and Drug Administration (FDA) but because they have been used safely over and over again by health care professionals.

The Misconception About "Natural" Treatments

That is not necessarily true for the myriad of alternative and natural approaches that some parents will opt for in lieu of corticosteroids and quick-relief medications. They assume that "natural" means safe, and the supplement and alternative-practice industry continually, and quite effectively, communicates that message. However, that is not the case.

Many natural treatments have not been thoroughly tested in controlled clinical trials, and their manufacture and processing are not regulated. The FDA only requires that supplement companies list their products' ingredients, and the Federal Trade Commission only insists that they not make misleading claims about effectiveness or their ability to cure disease. But determining what is "misleading" overstatement or sheer nonsense is essentially subjective, and many supplement companies stretch the truth. More to the point, their products are not backed up by proven science. Because they are sold over the counter and don't need FDA approval to be sold, they are not required to conduct well-designed, controlled clinical trials. There is no proof that they work in children or adults, and there are no studies to show that they work in asthma or any other disease. We also don't know if they are completely safe or have any side effects, and we can't be confident that they are free of contamination or impurities that can prove dangerous.

In the past several years, there have been several instances where natural treatments have been linked to serious health risks. Ephedra, taken for hunger management and weight loss and still promoted for treatment of asthma, was found to cause heart attack, strokes, and death. Bitter orange, which is marketed as a nasal decongestant and for weight loss, has been shown to cause increases in blood pressure in mice—not surprising, since the active ingredient, synephrine, is a stimulant. Manufacturers tried unsuccessfully to market a "skinny pill" for weight loss in children, but they were stopped when the U.S. Congress began investigating the development of the product and found that it had never been tested in children. Had it missed the attention of lawmakers, then a "natural" product that was in fact a type of diuretic or "water pill" could have been marketed and sold to parents who were unaware that the product contained ingredients linked to liver and kidney damage.

However, some natural remedies appear safe and have been used for years without harm. Vitamin C, for example, doesn't appear to be any real danger to children; and yoga, breathing exercises, acupuncture, and diets that include oily fish (in moderation) will most likely not do harm. Echinacea, a plant formulated into tablets, teas, and tinctures and often used to relieve symptoms from colds and other upper respiratory conditions, appears to be safe, although research has found it to be ineffective in treating common cold symptoms that can provoke an asthma episode. When the approach appears safe and parents want to try alternative methods or combine them with conventional approaches, I am typically all for it. I am—and believe other physicians should be—interested only in our patients getting well. When selecting the alternative option, however, parents need to ask themselves some hard questions.

When Parents Refuse Conventional Treatment

Parents who insist that their child eschew any drug treatment to get symptoms under control—limiting the management plan to natural remedies, environmental control, and perhaps immunotherapy—should ask themselves whether it is more beneficial to have their child treated with conventional medicines that have been proven safe and effective versus natural treatments that have not. If, after careful consideration, they decide that they want to use alternative approaches—either exclusively or along with conventional treatments—then as a physician, I respect that decision and support them, provided that their chosen alternative methods are not unhealthy or downright dangerous. We then move to a management plan that incorporates the alternative approaches with careful monitoring to ensure that their child is getting better.

Not infrequently, I have witnessed improvement in children who have not taken asthma drugs and instead have seen a chiropractor, Eastern medicine practitioner, or an acupuncturist, and they have gotten better. They may have combined these approaches with large doses of vitamins, minerals, herbs, and dietary and highly restrictive environmental controls that go well beyond what we recommend for children with asthma. The children seem to tolerate the therapy well, with no side effects. Some will continue to see me, others won't, but I am simply happy that the child feels better, even though I have no clear explanation as to why (perhaps the placebo effect played a role, which I will discuss further). In some cases, these children remain symptom-free; in many other cases, they do not. The symptoms return, and the parents bring their child back to see me, looking for guidance on their options.

When an Alternative Approach Is Not Working

In other cases, the child does not show significant improvement and will continue to have a nighttime cough, wheeze, or daytime symptoms. These symptoms may be reduced, but they are still present and keeping the child from experiencing the well-being and vitality that come with a good night's rest, energy, and the ability to feel competent and capable of taking on any activity. Daily asthma symptoms make that impossible for most children. And some parents who are adherents of an alternative philosophy are willing to tolerate these symptoms. I think, in these moments, it is again important to ask yourself what is best for your child.

It is perfectly reasonable to elect to try an alternative approach, but rationalizing its benefits—"a few symptoms are OK; she's really better"—does a child an injustice. It is worth giving alternatives a try if a parent feels strongly that a completely drug-free treatment plan should be explored. But if it fails to work—and frequent daily symptoms mean that it hasn't—then it is time to incorporate more conventional methods into the plan.

With the four-week proactive plan, parents remain involved and empowered throughout, and work with the physician to keep drug regimens as streamlined as possible. The goal, as always, is attaining and maintaining symptom freedom with as few drugs as possible.

Proceeding Cautiously with Alternatives

As a conventional physician, I take the unconventional view that alternatives are worth investigating and pursuing. If an alternative treatment was tested in well-designed, controlled clinical trials with enough participants to show a *statistical significance*—in broad terms, that means there are enough patients enrolled to ensure that the results are not caused by coincidence or statistical fluke—then I would recommend its use to patients immediately. The history of medical research has shown that true scientific progress that makes a difference in the lives of patients often comes unexpectedly. The discovery of penicillin from molded bread, the strides in heart attack and cancer treatment, and the discovery thirty years ago that asthma is a disease of inflammation changed the course of clinical practice.

With greater attention to the potential of alternatives, I suspect, we will at some point have the data to support use of complementary therapies in treating patients, including children. However, at this point, the data aren't strong enough or convincing enough (or in some cases aren't there because studies haven't been done in humans at all) to justify a recommendation, particularly when treating children.

Many alternative therapies are focused on combating inflammation and recognize it as a cause of many diseases, including asthma. While that underlying premise may be sound, the explanation of its impact has no scientific basis. Inflammation is seen as being caused by a broad array of foods, irritants, environmental fumes and odors, plastics, food additives, household products, synthetic fabrics, pesticides, gasoline, and car fumes. Yeast overgrowth is often cited as a contributing factor. Inflammation is seen as the direct result of immune system insult—that is, the constant bombardment of chemicals and so-called toxins in our air, water, households, and schools attacks our immune systems and damages the respiratory tract, the central nervous system, and other organs. The reasoning behind these theories, proposed disease mechanisms, and rationales has never been shown to have any scientific validity.

In some cases, asthma has been characterized as a disease of the nervous system, which harkens back to the days when children with asthma were told that it was "all in their head" and believed to have emotional or psychiatric problems. In this particular case, parents are told to purchase a spray that "kindly talks" to the nervous system and strengthens that subset of it that is deemed "weak" and given to provoke asthma attacks.

The sprays, supplements, and dietary regimens for dealing with this "toxic" onslaught are often expensive or extreme and difficult to carry out. Treatment may center on a highly restrictive or rotating diet that eliminates certain foods, then returns them to the diet, and then eliminates them again over several weeks, along with several supplements to be taken daily. It is complicated for parents and extremely boring and potentially harmful to children, who may not get enough nutrients. Parents may insist there is improvement, and I accept that assertion, but very often objective measures (e.g., spirometry, peak-flow measurements, or daily diaries of medication use and symptoms) show no improvement at all.

But while most alternative therapies have not been shown effective in childhood asthma treatment, and their value has not been tested in large-scale controlled clinical trials, there is some evidence from small studies to suggest that some may be proven beneficial in the future. Bear in mind that so far these studies haven't been conducted in children, so there is no evidence to show that they would realize a similar benefit. Still, some have shown promise and may have a place in a program that combines the best of alternative and complementary approaches.

The Alternative Arsenal: Potentially Valuable Treatments

In short, I divide alternative treatments into three categories: the "good," the "bad," and the "who knows? . . . but (probably) harmless." As studies continue and we learn more, these categories may shift. For example, some treatments previously thought to be harmless may be found to be otherwise, and some potentially helpful treatments may prove to be ineffective or harmful. With a greater emphasis on the study of alternative treatments, notably at the National Institutes of Health Center for Complementary and Alternative Medicine, we'll learn more and be able to more confidently assess the role of various alternative modalities within the childhood asthma management plan.

Until then, however, the benefits are anecdotal. Here are some treatments that fall, albeit cautiously, into my first category as being potentially valuable if additional, large-scale studies are conducted.

N-Acetyl Cysteine

One small Canadian study of a patient with an inflammatory lung disease found that she improved after adding a protein called N-acetyl cysteine (NAC) to her treatment regimen. NAC is converted in the body to glutathione, an antioxidant believed to protect the airways from the destructive effects of neutrophils, macrophages, and eosinophils—the immune system culprits that are part of the inflammatory cascade that provokes asthma episodes and worsens inflammation of the airways. We may find with further study that NAC may prove helpful in reducing inflammation in asthma, but at this point, one small study in an adult who suffered with chronic obstructive pulmonary disease and underlying asthma is not enough to recommend its widespread use.

Magnesium

Research has demonstrated that the mineral magnesium may have potential as an addition to an asthma treatment regimen, but further study is needed to determine whether it should be routinely added to asthma management plans. The studies with magnesium have been relegated to intravenous infusion of the mineral when asthma patients are hospitalized, and physicians often give it intravenously when patients are experiencing a serious asthma emergency.

In addition, researchers in England found that the lung function of adults improved when they increased their daily intake of magnesium, but the study population was random. In other words, it wasn't conducted in people with diagnosed asthma. At this point, there have been no studies done on the day-to-day use of magnesium supplementation in either adults or children with asthma. Any evidence showing that it can work is purely anecdotal—the medical term for physician word of mouth.

"Who Knows but (Probably) Harmless" Alternatives

My third category of alternative treatments is for those that appear to be harmless but have apparently no therapeutic benefit for asthma despite their popularity. While parents note symptom improvement when using some of these approaches, it may have more to do with the placebo effect and less to do with the treatment.

Often, parents will detail how their child is doing better with such approaches, and I am always delighted to hear it. I want my patients to get better, and I would be thrilled if we had conclusive data on the benefits of nonpharmacologic regimens. However, we don't have the data at this point, and moreover, the symptom improvement that children experience with the alternatives can be transitory or not demonstrated by objective tests. In other words, parents conclude that a child's symptoms have improved, and the child also may say that she feels better, but the diagnostic measurements of lung function fail to show any improvement. Again, in these instances, I believe it is the powerful placebo effect at work.

Placebos, generally sugar pills, are given as a standard control in clinical trials and often are found to work almost as well as the treatment itself. In fact, patients in most clinical trials who are assigned to the placebo "arm" experience a 25 to 30 percent improvement in symptoms simply because they believe that they should be improving. I don't discount the power and value of placebo, since feeling better is a tremendous gift, regardless of the route it takes. The downside of placebo, however, is that it is fleeting and tends to disappear as quickly as it came. Moreover, the complete reliance on symptoms may cover over the fact that underlying disease causes are not being addressed, thereby setting the patient up for a serious relapse.

In any case, the following therapies may not be therapeutically valuable, in my view, but they appear to be harmless and may prove of some value to parents, particularly when combined with more standard treatments.

Acupuncture

Most proponents of acupuncture insist that there are few diseases that it cannot effectively treat. The ancient Chinese practice has become popular in Western culture in recent years, and it is used exclusively by some practitioners and as an adjunct to medications, homeopathy, naturopathy, and psychotherapy. Many patients try acupuncture at some time for relief of asthma, allergic rhinitis, and allergic skin conditions.

Although some patients report temporary benefit, there have been no reported studies documenting either symptomatic improvement or long-term change in the course of either allergies or asthma. Furthermore, acupuncture may prove impractical in children, who might be willing to tolerate a quick prick for an allergy test or immunotherapy but may resist having needles remain in their skin for a half hour or more every few days.

Homeopathic Remedies

Homeopathy is an alternative form of healing based on the theory that "like" should be treated with "like," meaning that the cause of any disease should be treated with a small amount of the substance that actually causes the disease. Many parents like the idea of homeopathy, and in some ways, it does resemble allergy immunotherapy. The extracts are serially diluted through a process known as succession. There is no evidence that homeopathic remedies have any therapeutic value for any disease. There are no studies to show effectiveness in treating childhood asthma, but the remedies, which consist of extracts of a number of natural substances, including plants, animal products, and insects, are most likely harmless.

Fish Oils

A great deal of attention has been directed at fish oils that contain essential fatty acids known as omega-3s. These nutrients have been studied extensively for their potential in treating rheumatoid arthritis, diabetes, and prostate cancer, among other diseases. The anti-inflammatory properties of fish oils prompted some researchers to consider whether they held any promise for asthma treatment. However, a well-designed study determined that there was no benefit for asthma sufferers. Still, consuming high-quality fish in reasonable amounts cannot harm a child and can be included as part of a healthful diet in any child—or adult, for that matter. Fish oil supplements, while not providing any benefit in asthma, most likely won't cause harm.

Quercetin

The supplement quercetin is often prescribed by alternative practitioners for children and adults with asthma, although it has never been tested for its effectiveness in treating the disease. Quercetin is a bioflavonoid—a substance that causes pigments in plants and flowers. The rationale for using quercetin in allergic diseases, including asthma, is its apparent ability to prevent inflammation and act as an antihistamine. While neither claim has been documented, this substance is probably not harmful.

Ginkgo Biloba

The herb ginkgo biloba gained a fair amount of popularity several years ago for its supposed ability to treat Alzheimer's disease and other memory disorders, such as senility. While there has been some research to suggest a modest benefit in those types of diseases, the evidence of its ability to help asthma patients is scant. One small controlled study from Spain showed only modest benefit in adults. Still, ginkgo has not been shown to pose problems, and it appears to have no immediate side effects.

Vitamins and Minerals

Vitamins A, E, and A/beta-carotene have been studied extensively in asthma and results are inconclusive; some studies show symptom improvement and others show no improvement at all. Parents who want to incorporate these supplements into an overall treatment plan for their child should discuss it with their physician. None of these vitamins poses any harm and may be helpful; however, it is important to note that no studies have ever been conducted in children.

Other supplements—including slippery elm and licorice root and the minerals selenium, copper, and zinc—are embraced by some parents, with, again, no evidence that they are effective. However, there is no evidence to suggest they are harmful, so I won't actively try to stop parents from using them, provided that their child remains under the care of a physician who can monitor symptoms.

Troubling Alternatives

The risk that parents will forgo effective treatment in the instances when alternatives aren't working is among the most problematic issues I face as a physician. It is also among my greatest concerns when treating children. A parent's decision to try an exclusively nondrug approach to asthma treatment is fine—and one I can respect—as far as it goes. When children fail to improve, however, I am forced to put this approach in the "bad" column as, quite frankly, a decision that does not support a child's well-being. In addition to what I would call a blind spot with regard to alternative methods, I list several more in this section that fall into the category that I strongly urge parents to avoid because there are either questions or known facts about their safety risks. These alternatives are often recommended to parents of children with asthma, along with others who suffer from chronic conditions, but there is no evidence to show that they are in any way effective or safe.

Injection of Food Extracts

The injection of food extracts is a form of allergy immunotherapy directed at curing food allergy. The serious issue is that it is extremely dangerous and should never be used as a way to reduce food allergy for anyone at any time. As we've discussed, allergy immunotherapy is only undertaken to treat allergies caused by airborne allergens—such as pollens. When even small amounts of food extracts are given to reduce or eliminate food allergy, hives or dangerous anaphylaxis can occur. Some patients experience life-threatening anaphylactic reaction from even the smallest amounts of food allergen. Fatalities from food anaphylaxis have been reported most commonly in cases of peanut allergy. Peanut protein is found in a variety of foods, so that strict avoidance is difficult for even the conscientious patient.

Allergen immunotherapy to eliminate or reduce the anaphylactic sensitivity in IgE-mediated food allergy is currently undergoing investigation in controlled clinical trials, but it is far from becoming a reality. Nevertheless, some practitioners routinely prescribe food extract injections, often consisting of a combination of foods based on skin test results or patients' reports of intolerance to foods. This form of treatment must be considered unproved as to efficacy and a potential danger until appropriate clinical trials have been conducted.

Symptom-Relieving Neutralization

An approach called symptom-relieving neutralization is designed to counter the "world as enemy" disease often embraced in alternative circles. It uses a set of extracts consisting of allergens, foods, or chemicals to neutralize symptoms over the course of several months, proposing that these extracts will "fix" a faulty immune system. Parents are told to inject or give their child under the tongue a small amount of these neutralizing extracts to either relieve or prevent symptoms from environmental exposure.

As I mentioned previously, alternative approaches often see the root cause of allergies and asthma in the general environment and seek to neutralize its impact on the immune system. However, the range of allergies and sensitivities is typically extensive and unsubstantiated. Allergies, particularly those caused by food, are often implicated in asthma without undertaking an elimination process to pinpoint the chemical or food that provokes symptoms. The published studies of neutralization are either anecdotal or inadequate, and I suspect that any benefit is based on the power of suggestion.

Environmental Chemical Avoidance

Allergists recommend a reasonable program of allergen avoidance for patients with respiratory allergy. Simple measures to reduce exposure to house dust and dust mites through the elimination of bedroom carpeting and special casings for the bedding are clinically effective and, by and large, easy to implement. Similar measures can be taken to reduce indoor air levels of mold spores and other allergens.

In contrast, the concept of multiple food and chemical sensitivities comes complete with recommendation for extensive avoidance of environmental chemicals. Adherents to environmental chemical avoidance (called *idiopathic environmental intolerance*) fall in the same camp as the "neutralizers" in the efforts to combat a toxic world. To that end, these "environmentalists" recommend that patients avoid any exposure, even minute amounts, to multiple chemicals such as pesticides, organic solvents, vehicle exhaust fumes, gasoline fumes, household cleaners, glue and adhesives, new carpets, and many other substances. The problem, again, is that this kind of treatment unduly frightens people and sends them into a whirlwind of avoidance activity based on unproven, unfounded beliefs based on unproven diagnostic measures. There is no proof that these drastic measures are helpful. On the contrary, many physicians believe they could cause significant psychological harm.

When Dietary Changes Focus on More than Food Allergies

The only time that diet is a factor in treating asthma is when the asthma trigger is a documented food allergy. Such a distinction is important, since beyond a diagnosed food allergy, there is no evidence showing that dietary manipulation helps children with asthma. In fact, the problem with dietary restrictions is that they may create a condition called *failure to thrive*, which is caused by a child failing to get enough nutrients or enough of a particular type. Asthma is not diabetes. The only time you will see dramatic improvement is when food allergies are involved.

Eliminating Undiagnosed Food Allergies

Avoidance is the only certain method for treating food allergy. Although any food has the potential for being allergenic, food allergy is limited to one or at most a few foods. However, alternative practitioners often promulgate the unfounded theory of "food sensitivities"—in short, the "allergies" children supposedly have to wheat, dairy, sugars, food additives, and other substances—when no documented food allergy exists.

As we've noted, food allergies do affect a relatively small percentage of children with asthma. Airborne allergens pose a far greater risk and affect much larger numbers of children. With true food allergy (the common food allergies seen in children are to milk, wheat, soy, eggs, and peanuts) dietary restriction is necessary. However, the contention that a child has a "hidden" food allergy that has yet to be uncovered is often not factual. It does happen but, again, is limited to a handful of foods at most. Alternative practitioners sometimes support and encourage this thinking that children are "allergic" to many foods and food ingredients, which is not grounded in any evidence.

In truth, food allergy is relatively easy to diagnose, typically by a medically supervised test where the food is eliminated from a child's diet and symptoms are monitored. The reaction to a true food allergy is immediate, usually within minutes and definitely within one hour in most cases, and generally obvious. When parents suspect numerous food allergies, I will recommend an elimination diet, removing the food and then seeing if symptoms improve. I have embarked on this course with parents many times in my medical practice and have never found a "hidden" food allergy. Some parents believe strongly that their child harbors food sensitivities and allergies even when we simply can't find them. A broad range of food and beverages become suspect, and the risk of nutritional deficiency is obvious. However, in practice, many parents abandon these highly restrictive diets because of the difficulty of keeping children on such a punitive food regimen and because they see little benefit.

In short, imposing dietary restrictions makes sense only when a child has a documented food allergy or in early infancy when there is a strong family history of asthma or allergies. In the latter case, research suggests that women with a family risk for asthma breast-feed for at least six months, supplementing with hypoallergenic formula if necessary. In addition, they should delay the introduction of solid foods into the infant's diet until after the baby is six months old to potentially prevent asthma in their child. (The data also show that avoiding tobacco smoke while pregnant and reducing the child's exposure to dust mites and furry pets during the first year of life could lower the risk of developing asthma, as well.)

Rotary Diversified Diet

Proponents of the concept of multiple food allergies sometimes recommend a *rotary diversified diet*, in which the patient rotates foods so that the same food is eaten only once every four to five days. They may, for example, have their child eat soy products for a week, then avoid them for two weeks, then reintroduce them, all the while tracking apparent changes in symptoms. To do this, it is necessary to keep extensive and accurate food diaries, causing further unnecessary and time-consuming attention to diet and symptoms.

Eliminating or Reducing Dairy Products

Even in the absence of a milk product allergy, some parents will decide to eliminate dairy products from their child's diet. The explanation: dairy promotes mucus, and that is the last thing she needs. However, despite the commonly held belief that mucus production is the by-product of eating cheese or drinking milk, there is no evidence to suggest that dairy provokes increased mucus production. Some parents insist their child does better when dairy is removed or sharply reduced from the diet. In broad terms, I have no problem with this, but calcium would need to be replaced, and that is not easy to do with children, who will need to get it either through supplements or some green vegetables. My strong suggestion is that if your child hasn't been given a diagnosis of a dairy allergy, then don't restrict such an important mineral as calcium from her diet.

"Alternative" Tests

The tests that some alternative practitioners use to diagnose and treat asthma also have been shown to be highly suspect by some of the leading professional medical organizations in the country. The cytotoxic test, which is often used to diagnose allergies and asthma, has been discredited by the American Academy of Allergy, Asthma and Immunology and the National Center for Health Care Technology, which have issued statements claiming that the test lacks any scientific grounding. In the test, a sample of the patient's blood is placed under a microscope alongside a myriad collection of suspected allergens, food extracts, drugs, or chemicals for several hours. The slide is checked periodically to look for changes in the blood cells, with certain changes denoting an allergy or disease.

The problem with this test and similar ones is that they are both expensive and not effective in diagnosing disease. The cytotoxic test, for instance, cannot identify the presence of the true allergy and asthma mediators that are released during an asthma episode or the IgE antibodies that are present in children with allergies and asthma. Furthermore, it doesn't allow for the fact that cell changes on the slide could be caused by anything from temperature changes to contaminated food extract used on the slide. There are other diagnostic tests that claim to positively identify asthma and allergies in children, but they seem to be a justification for ongoing treatment. Parents may find that the original list of allergens and triggers that are bothering their children's asthma triples after they have seen an alternative practitioner.

Having been administered a diagnostic test, they are told that the child is not only allergic to pollen and nuts, but rather has a range of "allergies" and sensitivities that are causing her asthma, and that once eliminated, her asthma will be cured. As I've discussed, the impact is potentially damaging, with restrictive diets, unnecessarily complicated food regimens, and large doses of supplements. It adds a great deal of pressure and tension to an already tense situation—that of dealing with a chronic childhood disease.

It also sets up a dynamic between your child and the world that I find disheartening. Instead of helping her learn what she needs to do to embrace life—to enjoy it, live it fully, and do all that she needs and wants to do as a child and throughout adulthood—it identifies the world as "the enemy," filled with noxious chemicals and harmful invaders that will hurt her. Some threats to children and their well-being are indeed real—personal safety, safety on the Internet, and carefully crossing the street. There is no need to add more—and needless—worry to the mix.

The Placebo Effect

Many parents insist that various alternative treatments help tremendously, and as I discussed earlier, even I have witnessed the improvement myself. Children on a regimen of Chinese herbs, for example, may show signs of symptom relief (provided that environmental controls are firmly in place and adhered to at home and school), and I—along with their parents—are delighted. As a physician, I only want that my patients get better, even if I am not sure how it happens in these cases. My suspicion, with respect to some alternative treatments, is that the placebo effect takes hold and makes a huge difference in symptoms. The research on placebo effect is convincing: placebo effect, even in children, can prompt powerful symptom relief in patients. That is why patients receiving placebo pills in a controlled clinical trial will often show improvement along with those patients receiving a drug.

The trouble with placebo, however, is that its effect is often temporary. Symptoms, unfortunately, return, and parents are left to ponder their next steps. At this point, I often emphasize the value of incorporating conventional treatment into the management plan, even with ongoing use of the alternative treatment. I am extremely uncomfortable—and believe parents should be, as well—with ongoing symptoms. The impact of asthma symptoms diminishes a child's quality of life, which is important enough in itself, but the problem is even more far-reaching. Unchecked asthma symptoms affect school performance, social development, and a child's feelings of self-worth. Children and teens, as we've discussed, become depressed and anxious when asthma symptoms are part of daily life. And to compound the emotional impact, their airways are on their way to being permanently damaged—a phenomenon known as *airway remodeling*, in which the bronchial tubes are irreversibly changed in shape and ability to function. Symptoms that are unremitting and aren't addressed with an effective management plan end up damaging a child, literally, for life.

Proactive Asthma Care and Alternative Treatments

Although I am not an alternative practitioner, I generally support a parent's decision to incorporate complementary treatment into their child's plan. So if parents want to combine environmental controls and allergy immunotherapy, for example, with Chinese herbal remedies or acupuncture, I would place such approaches in my "who knows but (probably) harmless" category. I won't discourage them, as I have no knowledge that such approaches will hurt their child, and I will monitor her progress to make sure that she is moving toward a life without activity restriction or symptoms.

I welcome the dialogue, and I think that your pediatrician or general-practice physician should do the same. Often physicians feel unsupportive of alternative treatments and criticize in subtle and not so subtle ways a parent's decision to investigate them and incorporate them into a plan. In acknowledging that no data exist to support many of their claims, they dismiss a parent's interest or actively try to convince them that they are wrong to pursue complementary approaches.

The same fundamentals of proactive asthma care apply regardless of the issue being discussed. You as a parent deserve to be listened to and to have your questions, concerns, and interests respected. It is fine for physicians to disagree, and it is their responsibility to strongly discourage any practice that could pose a danger for your child. But dismissing alternatives out of hand is something you should question. Chances are, you will do what it is you think is best, but "hiding" your child's use of supplements, acupuncture, or other modality undermines the physician-parent partnership and, ultimately, your child's asthma progress. If you feel strongly about using alternatives and believe that you have not been heard by your physician, then you may, as in other instances when you may have felt ignored, choose to find a physician who is more open to your ideas and willing to explore how to combine alternatives and standard treatments.

In my experience, children with asthma gain a certain emotional depth and maturity that come from needing to accept rather early that life is not fair and that certain problems can't be wished away. This depth, in my view, comes from grappling with the disappointment and the initial fear of receiving a diagnosis of a chronic disease. It is then fostered by the child's resiliency and optimism, which we can continually foster.

That said, parents need honesty and support in dealing with these challenges. My concern with respect to alternative treatments is that so much of what is discussed and publicized as fact is, simply put, conjecture. It may be fine for adults to assume a certain risk in trying some new treatment or approach for ourselves, but we need to be extremely careful with the care of our children.

Additionally, parents should be told the whole story when it comes to alternatives in terms of the often overwhelming financial and logistical demands that make a difficult situation even harder. Alternative treatments for asthma are not covered by insurance companies, precisely because they are unproven. While some managed-care and insurance companies offer complementary medicine riders on employee-sponsored health plans, the coverage is limited to a handful of conditions that have been shown in clinical studies to respond to such treatments (typically chiropractic or acupuncture for some types of mild pain). Parents who elect alternative treatments have to pay all the costs out of pocket, which could be exorbitant. Since alternative treatment is ongoing, these costs could amount to thousands of dollars a year.

As a physician who has seen the power of conventional approaches and who has recognized the flaws in how we treat childhood asthma, I believe that proactive asthma care bridges the treatment gap. Rather than building on fear, worry, unfounded claims, and questionable safety issues, my program uses the best that we have to offer and gives parents and children the gift of a life focused on embracing its promise.

PART II

Taking Control: A Four-Week, Proactive Asthma Care Program

6

Week One

The Doctor's Office Exam, Exposed

WHEN YOU THINK of "history," it no doubt conjures up exhaustive high school lectures of facts, dates, and milestones. The textbooks and discussions may have focused on major social and political upheaval, as well as quieter events that ultimately emerged to have a significant impact on the period you were studying. A physician's history is not dissimilar to the history from your school years. It requires questioning, probing, and a pursuit of information and facts to gain a clear picture of any health issues.

A history, for a physician, is the essential element of the initial office visit. It is the framework for finding out what is happening, why it is happening, and what is to be done about it. It is how we come to understand your child's difficulties and appreciate the impact of his symptoms.

Without a solid and effective history, there is every chance that the diagnosis will be inaccurate or incomplete, only serving to prolong suffering and symptoms. Even if your child receives an asthma diagnosis, a history that is anything less than thorough could overlook important factors, such as triggers, or underlying allergies or other conditions, such as gastroesophageal reflux disorder (GERD) or sinusitis. Taking an ineffective history could, in some cases, hurt him further by prompting unnecessary diagnostic tests that lead to prescriptions for medication that does not help or that causes unnecessary side effects.

If your child's asthma symptoms are not improving after a couple of weeks, the initial history-taking is the first place to search for clues. However, that is only one aspect of the initial office visit to discuss his symptoms. The first office visit provides a blueprint for an ongoing partnership between you (and your child) and your physician, the office nurse, and other health care professionals. It is an opportunity to learn about childhood asthma, gain an awareness of the impact it is having and will continue to have on your child's life, and understand how to monitor his improvement.

In addition to prescriptions, you should leave the office with a basic understanding of asthma, an awareness of your child's specific asthma triggers, a suspicion of underlying allergies (and a plan to see an allergy/asthma specialist for future evaluation and comanagement, if warranted), and a diagnosis of other diseases associated with asthma that could be worsening symptoms. Make sure you have learned how to use an inhaler, a spacer or nebulizer, if needed, and a peak-flow meter to monitor his airway function. Your physician should also have provided you with samples or enough refills on the prescriptions so that you—or the pharmacist—do not have to call the physician's office every month for refills. Make sure you have been given information on where to purchase asthma devices. To make it easier for my patients, I maintain a small inventory of all necessary devices, which they can purchase before they leave the office.

In Chapter 4, I reviewed the asthma medications and kinds of drug combinations that are often given, depending on the severity of your child's disease, in order to aggressively treat symptoms in the beginning, with a goal toward decreasing dosages over time. In addition to medication, you should have left the office with a confidence in your and your child's ability to use asthma devices and to monitor his breathing daily with a peak-flow meter. As a true partner, your physician or nurse should have given you brochures, website information, and articles on childhood asthma and expected that you will have "boned up" on asthma and read them by the next office visit. And, like a partner, you should have been given an e-mail address or fax number to keep in frequent contact with your physician on your child's symptoms.

If the office visit was less than comprehensive, then the proactive asthma care approach will provide you with the tools and skills you need to fill in those gaps. This is a critical step if your child hasn't improved significantly since the initial office visit. Our first step is to review the history-taking, review the questions your child's physician should have asked, and then discuss what to do if she failed to address certain aspects of your child's health and asthma symptoms.

A Lesson in History: What Should Be Covered in the Initial Office Visit

First-time asthma office visits are overwhelming for many parents, and understandably so. You've just heard that your child has a chronic and serious disease, and you're rushed through an explanation of treatment and perhaps received a pamphlet on children and asthma. You're told to make a return visit in two weeks and to call the office if there are any problems. You may find it challenging to recall what the physician asked during the history-taking. But reflecting on the visit and remembering as much as possible will prove helpful in getting to the bottom of the obstacles that are getting in the way of your child's improvement.

The following sections provide a list of things that your physician should have asked and discussed with you during the history and are critical to an accurate diagnosis and creation of an effective treatment plan but often are overlooked.

Risk Factors: Prematurity, Allergies, and Intolerances

Did the doctor ask about birth factors, such as trauma and prematurity? We know that prematurity is a risk factor for asthma in infants and young children. Prematurity should be discussed and followed up with questions to determine the impact of a preterm birth, if any.

Also, did the physician ask about food allergies or intolerances, eczema, and lung infections in infancy? All three, as covered previously, are strong risk factors for developing asthma in childhood. Food allergies and eczema often precede asthma (the sequence known as the "atopic march"), and lung infections in infancy, such as respiratory syncytial virus (RSV), often predate asthma in children.

A "New" Risk Factor: Obesity

Obesity—at any age—has been emerging as one of the major public health issues of the early twenty-first century. However, it is only now being recognized as both a risk factor for asthma in children and a predictor that its symptoms will continue throughout adolescence. Obesity has increased more than 100 percent in children from 1980 to 1994, which, interestingly, is the same increase as was seen in childhood asthma rates. The reasons are not unlike those in adults and include lack of physical activity and exercise as well as supersized portions in restaurants and fast-food chains.

In children and adolescence, the influence of stationary, sedentary activities—such as computer games—makes it difficult for them to get the physical activity they need to burn off calories. This inactivity, coupled with the culture's love affair with salty, fried foods, junk foods, and sugary foods and beverages, makes it hard for any American to lose weight and keep it at a healthy level.

This issue poses a particular problem for children with asthma or for those who may be predisposed to developing it. New findings show that obesity often precedes asthma development in children: the more a child's weight increases, the greater the risk. In addition, asthma overall is more prevalent in obese children, and unless they are able to get their weight down to a healthy level, they are more likely to struggle with symptoms throughout adolescence versus children who are of a normal weight. It has also been found that if children with asthma lose weight, symptoms improve.

The findings on obesity are provocative and important, and more research needs to be done to determine how and why obesity plays a role in increasing asthma risk in children and making it worse. Some researchers suspect that the lack of physical activity in obese children may be the culprit. This suspicion is supported by increasing evidence that shows that a sedentary life for any child with asthma is counterproductive and contributes to increased severity of symptoms and more cases of asthma overall. The health benefits of exercise are well documented and familiar to virtually everyone, and in children with asthma, they may hold even greater benefits. Children with asthma who are physically active:

- Seem to need less medication
- Appear to have fewer emergency department visits
- Have less fear of exercise
- Experience reduced anxiety
- Are less likely to miss school due to asthma symptoms

Sadly, obese children tend to avoid exercise because of their weight, making them less likely to lose it. If your child is overweight or obese, it is important that you add this to the list of issues to discuss with his physician. Work out a plan for healthful eating and exercise, and set a goal for reaching a healthy weight for him that is reasonable and never punitive or extreme. While researchers continue to search for a cause-and-effect relationship, he will begin reaping the benefits of feeling better and, potentially, getting better control of asthma symptoms.

Discussion of Symptoms

Did the doctor discuss symptoms and, more importantly, ask more questions about coughing rather than wheezing? One of the most common errors made by family physicians and pediatricians is the overreliance on wheezing as a definitive asthma clue. Many babies experience wheezing, but not all go on to develop asthma (although some do). Coughing, however, is a major asthma symptom and is often dismissed as "just a cough" or a symptom of the common cold. Importantly, even if your child was diagnosed with asthma at the first visit, your physician should have asked several questions about the nature of the cough, whether it occurred at night, during exercise or play, or in the morning, to determine the best treatment approach.

Detection of Asthma Triggers

Did the doctor ask about when symptoms get worse—after viral infections, contact with fumes, smoke, construction particles, dogs, cats, or other furry pets, dust, after or during exercise, when the weather changes? Determining your child's asthma triggers, those allergens or irritants that prompt the airways to overreact and set the stage for an asthma episode, can take some careful detective work, but the knowledge is essential to his health.

Avoiding and minimizing triggers is an essential component of asthma prevention, and you need to review the possible triggers with your physician up front, so that you can deal with the issue wherever and whenever it arises. If you notice that your child's asthma symptoms get worse while at a friend's house, for example, you should ask whether the friend's family has furry pets or whether certain types of foods are eaten there that your child may not consume anywhere else. Perhaps his symptoms become markedly worse in the spring and fall, during camp or summer vacation, or after spending time outdoors in cold weather. Young children with recurrent upper respiratory infections and wheezing are often misdiagnosed as having a cold or cough. If you feel that some triggers may have been overlooked in the first office visit, review the checklist of asthma symptom triggers and discuss your concerns with the physician.

Discussion of Your Child's Environment

Did your physician ask about wood-burning stoves, cigarette smokers, or wood-burning fireplaces? Did you review whether symptoms worsen or improve when your child's environment changes (e.g., a different

Asthma Symptom Triggers Checklist

- Are symptoms year-long, seasonal, or both?
- Are symptoms continual, occasional, or both?
- How many days per week or month do symptoms occur?
- Do symptoms happen at home, school, day care, or all three?
- At what time of day, especially nighttime or early morning, do symptoms occur?
- Do symptoms occur after exercising or physical activity?

home, a different city, certain buildings—day-care center, for example) for clues about asthma triggers? Such a discussion requires careful thought, along with the recognition that environments outside the home are often laden with triggers that go undetected. For example, up to 30 percent of all homes and schools show the presence of cat dander, even if there are no cats on the premises. The dander has traveled on clothing and other materials into the environment.

Cleaning up a child's environment is another critical stop on the road to a symptom-free life. Frequently, an "environmental assessment" is overlooked at the first office visit and may never get addressed thoroughly at all. But making changes to your child's environment at home, school, day care or preschool, after-school activities, and clubs—in fact, anywhere he spends time—is extremely important.

Take time, even if your physician didn't, to think about all possible irritants that your child may come in contact with in and out-

Things That Make Your Child's Symptoms Worse

- Viral upper respiratory infections (colds and flu)
- Time indoors or at day care, school, preschool, church, etc. (possible allergy to mold, dust mites, animal dander)
- Time outdoors (possible allergy to pollen)
- Exercise, sports, physical activity
- Vacation (time in another home, at camp, etc.)
- Exposure to irritants (such as tobacco smoke, strong odors, or fumes from cleaning products, perfumes or sprays, air pollutants or smog)
- Strong emotions, such as fear, anger, frustration, crying, or laughing
- Changes in weather, temperature, or humidity
- Exposure to cold air
- For older children, menstruation, or irritants or chemicals used in part-time jobs

side the home. Use the symptom checklist on page 92 as a guide, and take it to your next office visit for discussion with your health care professionals.

Health care professionals should be aware of all of the environmental irritants in your child's life and should offer support and strategies for avoiding them whenever possible. I will spend considerable time in discussing strategies for managing irritants in and outside the home in Chapter 7, but the first step is knowing what the common asthma irritants are and making immediate plans to address those in your control. If you or another member of the family smokes, for instance, now is the time to quit (regardless of whether the physician discussed it during the office visit), and thought must be given to avoiding homes where people do smoke or use fireplaces or wood-burning stoves.

Diagnosis of Possible Other Conditions

Did the doctor suggest pursuing or diagnosing other conditions: GERD, sinus infections, chronic ear or other infection, which may worsen asthma symptoms? Did he ask about other diseases or conditions that often exist alongside asthma, such as hay fever, eczema, and food allergies? As we've learned, the failure to treat conditions that produce or worsen asthma symptoms will keep your child from improving. Make sure that your physician has ruled out these conditions or, if not, properly diagnoses them and then takes action.

While your child may not have eczema or GERD, he may have allergic rhinitis (hay fever) or sinusitis. Both are common in children with asthma and, if undiagnosed or untreated, will make it difficult to control asthma symptoms. Typically, indoor and outdoor nasal allergies can be treated effectively with a nonsedating antihistamine (available over the counter) or nasal antihistamine and/or nasal steroid.

Referral to an Allergy Specialist

Did the physician recommend that you see an allergy specialist for further evaluation? If your child's pediatrician or family physician suspects allergies but is unsure, then he must refer you to an allergy specialist. It takes specific training to administer and interpret allergy test results. The American Academy of Pediatrics recommends that pediatricians arrange with allergy and asthma specialists in their communities to collaborate and comanage the child with asthma. The results of testing are usually available within fifteen minutes, and skin-testing results can be assessed immediately in the specialist's office. You will leave there with a relatively good picture of whether your child has allergies and, if so, which ones and what to do about them, along with a comprehensive management plan, enhanced understanding of your child's condition, and an awareness of environmental triggers. The specialist will comanage your child's asthma with your pediatrician.

Tests for Older Children

If your child is over age five, did the doctor check lung function with a breathing machine (*spirometer*)? Did she discuss the severity of the asthma symptoms based on the results of the test? A thorough medical history should offer very strong clues as to whether a child has asthma and how severe it is, and whether other conditions may be aggravating the disease.

However, history is not enough. The physician's assessment must be confirmed by what we call *objective measure*, that is, tests that measure the airflow into and out of your child's lungs. This measurement is done by use of a spirometer, a small computerized machine attached to a hose, and the testing is called spirometry. Your child breathes into the hose, and the machine measures the volume of air your child exhales. Then he should have been asked to inhale quick-acting medication, wait fifteen minutes, and undergo spirometry again to determine the degree to which airflow can be improved (i.e, how much the asthma obstruction can be reversed) with treatment. By assessing these measurements against the criteria for normal airflow, your physician can determine the severity of your child's asthma. Your physician should then access these measures against normal lung function to determine the severity of his asthma. This measurement is an essential component of the diagnostic process and is helpful in classifying asthma severity by national guidelines.

However, it is usually not possible to perform spirometry in children under age four. If your child is an infant or toddler, then your physician may need to diagnosis asthma based on empirical observation, symptoms, and/or the response to asthma therapy.

Understanding of Peak-Flow Meters

Were you and your child told to use a peak-flow meter, and, if so, were you given instructions on its importance and how to use it? A peak-flow meter is a small, portable device that monitors *peak expiratory flow* (PEF), or the amount of air that your child can exhale in one-tenth of a second. In general, most children age five and older can master it with relative ease. You should learn how to use the peak-flow meter in the physician's office.

It is particularly important to use a peak-flow meter daily in the first four weeks of treatment, as it provides an objective assessment of how your child is doing and can alert you to any problems that an asthma episode may be approaching. Ideally, your child should take a reading every morning before using any medication and in the late afternoon. A greater than 20 percent difference between the morning and evening measurements suggests inadequately controlled asthma. The following steps summarize how to use a peak-flow meter for effective results.

1. Use the meter twice a day: in the morning after your child wakes up but before he takes his asthma medication, and in the late afternoon or early evening before he takes any medication.
2. Move the marker on the meter to the bottom of the numbered scale.
3. Ask your child to stand up or sit up straight, take a deep breath, and fill his lungs completely.
4. He should hold his breath while you place the mouthpiece in his mouth, between his teeth. He should close his mouth around the mouthpiece.
5. He should blow out as hard and as fast as he can.
6. Write down the number that the marker is on (provided your child didn't make a mistake or cough, in which case he should repeat the process).
7. Repeat steps 1 through 3 two more times so that you have three numbers.
8. Your child's peak-flow number is the highest number of the three.

By monitoring breathing over the course of three to four weeks, you and your child will determine his personal best. The personal best is the average of the morning and afternoon readings recorded when your child does not have symptoms (typically beginning at the end of the first week) through the end of the third week. To get an accurate personal-best number, write down your child's morning and evening peak-flow numbers every day (a notebook or calendar works best) for three weeks. At the end of three weeks, add up the numbers, and then divide that sum by the number of readings you have. That is his personal best.

Once established at the end of the third week, your child's daily peak-flow reading should be 80 to 100 percent of his personal best. You would determine that percentage by dividing his daily number into his personal-best number. For example, let's say your child's personal best is 200, and his daily number is 150. You would divide 150 by 200 (use a calculator to ensure that you are accurate), and you will get 0.75 or 75 percent. This number would tell you that your child is five percentage points below his personal best, and he may need an adjustment in his medication or—together with you—a thorough assessment of whether you are both doing all you can to manage asthma triggers. In any case, you should call your physician, discuss the reading, and determine what is to be done about it. Normal peak-flow readings vary by height. The morning peak-flow reading is usually lower than the evening reading. Table 6.1 lists normal peak-flow readings by height.

Inclusion of Your Child in His Treatment and Care

Did the doctor speak directly to your child, ask questions, and teach him how to use the nebulizer, inhaler, and peak-flow meter? One of the most pervasive and disturbing problems in asthma care has nothing to do with diagnosis or medications, but it has a profound impact on your child's well-being now and throughout his life. It is our bias, as adults, in failing to include children in actively participating in their own care and symptom improvement.

As physicians and parents, we may tell children they have asthma and remind them to take medications, but we rarely involve children directly in their own care. With our cursory explanations, we may think that we are protecting children from disturbing information that

Table 6.1 Mean Normal Peak-Flow Values in Children

Height	Peak Flow	Height	Peak Flow
43 inches	147	56 inches	320
44 inches	160	57 inches	334
45 inches	173	58 inches	347
46 inches	187	59 inches	360
47 inches	200	60 inches	373
48 inches	214	61 inches	387
49 inches	227	62 inches	400
50 inches	240	63 inches	413
51 inches	254	64 inches	427
52 inches	267	65 inches	440
53 inches	280	66 inches	454
54 inches	293	67 inches	467
55 inches	307		

will trouble them, but in my view, the reverse is true. Keeping children out of the loop regarding their care, their symptoms, and the implications of asthma adds to anxiety and frustration, and what's worse, it makes controlling asthma symptoms more difficult.

In truth, children as young as age two can begin to learn about their asthma, but certainly any child over the age of eight can actively participate in his asthma care. Proactive asthma care is for parents and children, designed to empower both of you to gain control over asthma symptoms, rather than have the disease control you. It doesn't diminish the parents' caring or your involvement; rather, it helps ensure that your child can get the help he needs at school, day care, or a friend's house, because he has learned to be active, rather than passive, when it comes to his asthma and to take steps to take care of himself.

There is no reason to present the information in an alarming or overly dire tone. Instead, the news can be delivered with a straightforward, caring approach that conveys the truth—that asthma is serious but that it can be controlled if you, your child, and your physician all work together as a team. Your child needs to know that he is being taken care of and that the adults in his life are equipped to help him through difficulties. But he also can benefit from understanding his asthma and putting the disease into proper perspective. For example, he should understand that, yes, he will have to take medications, be aware of triggers, and work with adults to try to avoid them; and no, he will not have to give up activities that he wants to do, provided he works together with you and the physician to keep symptoms under control.

Availability and Scheduling of Follow-Up Visits

Did your physician schedule a follow-up visit within a week? Physicians who treat asthma need to be available, particularly on weekends and in the early morning and evening hours—as these are times when asthma episodes are more likely to occur. You should never feel, or be made to feel, intrusive or annoying because you are calling at an inconvenient time. In fact, physicians treating asthma should regard such calls as opportunities not only to help, but to learn more about problems with the treatment plan or medication.

Similarly, children with asthma need regular appointments, particularly in the early stages of treatment. No more than one week should pass between the first and second visit, and weekly visits need to continue for at least a month. Asthma's unpredictability and seriousness demand attention early on. Moreover, both of you need to gain confidence in using asthma monitoring and inhalation devices and a greater awareness about your child's symptoms, improvement, and trouble signs. This is not a job that can be taken on alone. You need the active involvement and guidance of a health care professional as you begin the treatment program and continue to adjust it over time. Asthma care is not a one-shot deal by any means, and waiting two or three weeks to see or speak to a physician is far too long a time to meet face-to-face and review progress or problems.

Proactive Asthma Care: The Office Visit, Revisited

What if your initial doctor's office visit left you with more questions than answers? If, after reading this chapter, you are concerned that you and your child did not get all of the attention and explanation that you needed, and if you're still feeling confused or uncertain about the treatment plan, medications, and other aspects of your child's asthma, then it is time to take action.

Develop a List of Questions

During this first week, you need to develop a list of questions to ask, along with any concerns you or your child have.

- Are you still uncertain about whether you are using the inhaler properly?
- Is your child still coughing at night?
- Are you worried that he may not have immediate access to an inhaler during the school day and have trouble again during physical education class?

These are the kinds of questions you may need to ask, but the list depends on your own individual concerns. No question is dumb, and no concern is ridiculous. Even if you asked the question at the office visit, it is fine—in fact, it is a good idea—to ask for clarification. The complexities of asthma, the challenges of day-to-day care, and the chronic nature of the disease make asthma a difficult condition to comprehend and navigate. It would be virtually impossible for any parent to get all the facts straight in one quick doctor's visit.

Once you have made a list of questions and concerns, jot them down so you won't forget any of them. Ask your child to add his questions to the list or to join you in formulating and writing the list. Just as with your concerns, his are valid and important. And, moving forward, always have paper and a pen handy whenever you speak with your child's physician. Bring both with you to all office visits, and take notes during telephone meetings. It is very easy to forget important information and guidance or to find yourself unsure or confused— there may be a lot to absorb. Writing the information down means not having to commit it to memory.

Contact Your Physician and Get Answers to Your Questions

Then contact the physician's office, and ask to speak with a member of the medical team (a nurse, nurse practitioner, or physician assistant).

In an emergency, you should speak to a member of the team, preferably the doctor, directly. He may not be able to speak with you immediately if he is seeing another patient, but he should call you back as soon as possible. Some physicians set aside a portion of the day to return patients' phone calls. Ask the receptionist when the doctor is expected to call back, and give the number where you can be reached during that time period. Giving two numbers, a home or office number and cell phone number, is helpful, along with a direction on which number should be called first.

Once you have the physician on the phone, ask your questions and listen carefully. You not only want to make sure you are actively listening to the responses, but also want to ask for further clarification if the explanations still strike you as confusing or vague. End the call with a thank-you, and note that you would like your child to have another appointment—every week for the next month or until symptoms resolve. Your physician should graciously accept your decision through agreement or encouragement.

Make Weekly Contact for the First Month

You may find that your child's doctor is less than enthusiastic about a weekly appointment. He may ask that you schedule a visit in two weeks, and you may be tempted to go along with fewer visits. While physicians are certainly time-crunched, it is important to have a weekly visit or at least weekly contact in the first four weeks of treatment. Once your child's asthma is stabilized, then you can reduce the number of visits to about one every three months in the first year (barring any problems or developments that need medical attention).

The first four weeks require more aggressive treatment to get symptoms under control, and this accelerated approach requires active physician involvement. There are factors specific to your child's asthma progress during this period that cannot be assessed over the phone, via fax, or e-mail. In short, the physician needs to:

- See your child
- Perform a spirometry
- Review and reinforce with you the importance of daily peak-flow monitoring, taking medication, and adjusting medications if necessary

He or the nursing staff needs to provide a refresher on how to use asthma medication and monitoring devices, and they need to ask pointed questions about symptoms over the past week.

Waiting two weeks to address problems with using an inhaler or managing ongoing symptoms is far too long to wait; it is one of the reasons why children don't experience sufficient progress in controlling asthma symptoms in the early treatment stages. The gap in office visits is inconsistent with the need for aggressive symptom control. This gap leaves children and parents with too much time without the support they need to feel confident that medications, devices, and monitoring equipment are being used properly.

It is rare for a doctor to deny a patient more frequent visits, so you should have no problem scheduling weekly ones for the first month. If questioned by the office staff or physician, you can simply say that in the first weeks of treatment, you feel that you and your child need more active involvement from the medical team. If you find that you simply can't get a doctor to agree to a weekly visit, then consider changing physicians. It may seem like a drastic move, but it speaks to a larger issue—that of the staff relating to you and your child as partners in care. You may not want to make a change immediately, as switching physicians is a decision that should not be made lightly. But you should consider a reluctance to schedule weekly up-front asthma visits as a sign that you could confront other types of resistance along the way. Chapter 9 deals in greater depth with how and when to switch physicians, but that decision will be driven by your doctor's response to your requests for help, support, or involvement.

Week One at Home: The Start of a Journey

Week one can be stressful for parents and children, but it can offer some relief from the incessant anxiety of not knowing what is wrong with your child. By seeing a physician and getting a proper diagnosis, you now know what you are dealing with and have the framework to turn around an out-of-control situation. But unlike many other conditions, with asthma, a diagnosis and prescriptions aren't enough to make lasting changes. As a chronic disease in children, it involves specific challenges and issues that you and your child will have to confront and manage. You will need to do this with the support of your physician and her medical team, including nurse educators, physician assistants, and nurses—as well as ancillary health care professionals that factor into your child's life, such as school and day-care nurses, pharmacists, camp medical personnel, and others. *Asthma is simply not a disease that can be managed in isolation.* It is a community issue as well as a personal one.

That said, asthma management does begin at home. At the first visit, you should have received several important pieces of information and directions described in the following sections to set you and your child on a symptom-free path immediately.

Gather All the Information You Need

Call it a crash course in asthma, but your physician's office should have provided you with a file full of brochures, websites, and other materials to help both of you understand asthma and its impact on the airways. If you didn't receive enough information to satisfy your questions and concerns, the information in Part I of this book will help fill those information gaps. In addition, there are countless patient education tools, including books, pamphlets, websites, and computer games designed to teach parents and children all they need to know about asthma.

I hope this book has already provided you with a firm footing in asthma, but additional materials, importantly those geared to children, can be extremely helpful in your child's acceptance of and knowledge of asthma. The Resources section at the end of this book offers a list of some of the best children's computer games, websites, and books for various ages that help a child make sense out of asthma and provide information that is understandable, reassuring, and enjoyable.

Develop an Asthma Management Plan

An asthma management or treatment plan will serve as your guide for putting your child on a symptom-free road. Your physician may give you a copy of a plan or diary for you to use each week, or you may decide to create your own. The management plan should include:

- A rundown of medications your child needs to take, the dosage, and when the medication should be taken
- Guidelines for what to do if symptoms worsen
- A section to record peak-flow readings and information about asthma triggers specific to your child

The most effective management plans adopt a "traffic light" approach (shown in Figure 6.1), with Green, Yellow, and Red Zones corresponding to your child's asthma status. These simple one-page charts are a memory aid for children as well as parents.

- **The Green Zone:** This is the zone where you always want your child to be—free of symptoms and without any restrictions on activities.
- **The Yellow Zone:** In this zone, asthma symptoms are getting worse, or your child is relying on quick-relief medication to keep his airways open. Steps should be taken immediately to reverse the trend—for example, increasing the frequency of the short-acting beta-2 agonist or starting a course of oral corticosteroid. If nothing works, call your physician within a prescribed number of hours to discuss the problem and quickly determine the next steps. If your child is in the Yellow Zone, he will be coughing or wheezing or waking up during the night due to asthma symptoms. He may be unable to do some activities. If he remains in the Yellow Zone for more than twenty-four hours or if symptoms get worse, then he is in the Red Zone, and you are in an emergency situation.
- **The Red Zone:** This zone signals a serious problem that needs immediate attention. If your child is in the Red Zone, he will have extreme shortness of breath and be unable to do his usual activities. You may see that his lips or fingernails turn blue or he has trouble walking. Some children in the Red Zone can be treated by giving larger or more frequent doses of short-acting quick-relief medication, but often they need to be taken to the emergency department.

Your management plan will be tailored to your child's treatment, and it will guide you through a series of quick assessments to know when and how quickly to take steps to address your child's symptoms. For example, if your child is in the Yellow Zone, experiencing symptoms, some nighttime wakefulness, and unable to participate in gym

Figure 6.1 Sample Green, Yellow, and Red Zone Asthma Management Plan

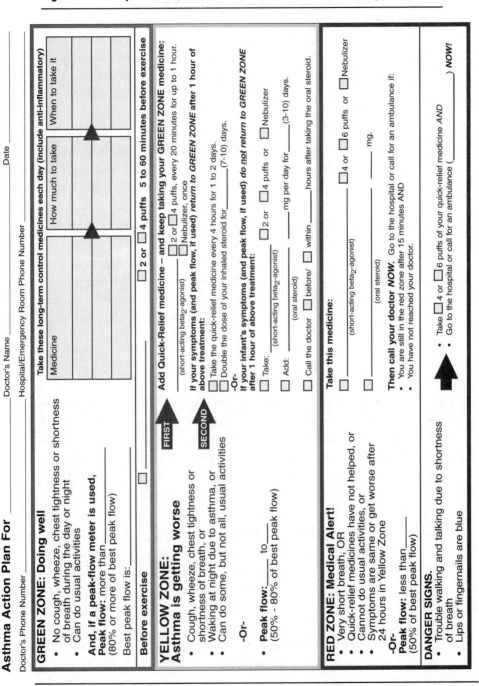

class, then you might add a quick-relief medicine through an inhaler and wait one hour to see if symptoms improve. If they do improve, then your plan may call for him to continue to take the quick-relief medication every four hours or so for a couple of days or to double the dose of inhaled corticosteroid for four to five days. If symptoms don't improve, then you might add an oral corticosteroid for three to ten days until symptoms improve.

The management plan should make it easy for you to know what to do and when to do it. If you never received a plan or if its directions are unclear, then ask for clarification from your physician. It is particularly important to have a clear management plan at the start of your child's treatment, as you are getting comfortable with the medications, learning how and when to deliver them, and identifying your child's specific asthma triggers.

Ideally, the physician or nursing staff should have put the plan together as the result of some in-office collaboration, so that it made sense for your and your child's routine. If it conflicts with either of your schedules, then it needs to be redrafted to incorporate the realities of your lives.

Asthma Management in More than One Household

If you are a separated or divorced parent, then you must ideally involve your ex-spouse in your child's asthma management. If you have a coparenting arrangement and your former spouse is actively involved in your child's life, then you should both accompany him on the next physician visit, to make sure that both of you understand the management plan, gain clarity and guidance on any issues regarding medication and asthma inhalation devices, and are in sync regarding the monitoring and assessment of his symptoms. It is particularly important that your ex-spouse be aware of asthma triggers and as diligent in helping your child avoid them as you are, and it is equally important that both of you recognize when your child may be moving into a Yellow Zone.

I can understand the complications and the frustrations of managing your child's asthma in two different households and in having to be in contact on a frequent basis—particularly at the start of his asthma treatment—with someone from whom you are separated or divorced. However, your child's health is paramount, so it is vital that you both work together as a team, regardless of how difficult or uncomfortable that might be.

Asthma Management for Working Parents

If you are a working parent, you will also no doubt be confronted with the challenges of asthma treatment. If your child is in day care or preschool, then you must involve the day-care nurse or caregivers in his asthma care. Similarly, if your child is in school, the school nurse must know he has asthma, have a copy of the management plan, and be able to provide him with support and medication should he require immediate attention during the day.

Of course, you would leave the day care or school with emergency contact numbers, but the nursing personnel will need to spring into action if your child requires emergency treatment. Therefore, you need to make sure that they have any written permissions they require, along with detailed information on his condition, triggers, medications, and devices. In Chapter 8, I will discuss in detail how to effectively forge a partnership with school nurses and others—including coaches and camp counselors—who supervise your child or are otherwise the person in charge if he needs assistance. But, when considering the care of your child and what you need from his physician, consider the entirety of his life, and make sure that the asthma management plan makes sense for your family.

Integrate Treatment into Your Own and Your Child's Life

The fundamentals of asthma management probably cannot and should not be altered, specifically monitoring, medication, and regular physician visits, but within the framework, there are many ways to address particular issues or lifestyle demands. For example, medication regimens can almost always be configured to correspond to the child's school day, and pharmacists in most states can—with a note from a physician—dispense medications in two separate bottles for separated or divorced parents.

In short, your child's asthma management plan needs to work for everybody. Parent and child should be actively involved in developing it from the first office visit, and that involvement should have also included agreed-upon asthma treatment goals—such as no missed school days, no more sleepless nights, and no limitations on activities. Ideally, both parents and caregivers should have received an up-front education on asthma, but at a minimum, you should feel that you have a solid background in the specifics of asthma, your child's condition, trigger avoidance, and actions to take immediately to get symptoms under control in all aspects of his life. The steps you and your child take to fill any information gaps early are the first steps of proactive asthma care.

7

Week Two

Charting Progress and Eliminating Asthma Triggers

QUITE A LOT is said about the American need for instant gratification. When it comes to health and well-being, we're often chided for our ceaseless attraction to "miracle cures"—quick fixes for everything from baldness to obesity. As a society, we often scold ourselves for demanding immediate results.

However, in my experience, parents of children with asthma don't fit this description. Often, they are far too tolerant, far too patient, and far too willing to adopt a wait-and-see attitude when it comes to their child's improvement. The reasons for this misplaced patience are complex, but I believe that it has much to do with the nature of the patient-physician relationship. The traditional relationship held to a top-down dynamic, with physicians holding the control and authority over treatment and disease management and patients highly dependent upon and directed by a physician's decisions.

To be sure, the consumerization of health care, in which patients play a more active role in their health and the health of their children, has altered this dynamic permanently, but remnants of it remain. Many people, in my experience, are reluctant to question and to find out more about their symptoms, side effects of medication, their disease prognosis, how to take their medicines, and more because they may feel intimidated or passive in the physician's office. Those remnants are also operative in managing childhood diseases, and for a completely under-standable reason: many parents assume that if there were something important they should know about, their doctor or some member of the health care team would tell them. However, as I discussed in ear-lier chapters, the health care system and physician education combine to make that assumption wrong in many cases.

In addition, many parents feel even more vulnerable and anxious when it comes to their children than when the health issues are their own. Our children depend upon us, and we hold an enormous respon-sibility in caring for them. This responsibility often results in parents being even more cautious, less willing to question, and more reticent with health care professionals who treat their children. But as I have also discussed, asthma is a disease that demands patient and parent involvement. The course of the disease and the ability to live a symp-tom-free life is tied to the active involvement of parents and children in proactive asthma care. When it comes to your child's asthma, there is no place for passivity—for either you or her. *Week two of your asthma plan is the time to put proactive asthma care into action.*

The Week Two Office Visit

So how is your child doing in week two, and what should you expect regarding symptoms?

- You should have already begun to see the benefits of treat-ment, and symptoms should be noticeably reduced.
- Your child should have very little need for the quick-relief inhaler (no more than twice a week or before exercise).
- There should be less or no wheezing, coughing, chest tight-ening, or other familiar signs.
- Your child should not feel the need to restrict activities because of asthma, and she should be feeling better overall, with more energy.

If things are going well, then there is no need to change the treat-ment plan. You should keep monitoring with the peak-flow meter and taking medications as prescribed.

At your second doctor's visit in week two, you should bring:

- Devices—metered dose inhaler, spacer, nebulizer
- Peak-flow meter
- All medications
- Completed asthma management plan
- A list of notes, questions, or concerns from either you or your child
- Paper and pen to take notes

You don't want to forget to ask about anything that is on your or her mind or have found confusing or complicated in the first week.

Your concerns at the week two visit may include when is the best time to have your child take medications and how to fit monitoring and recording the results of a peak-flow meter reading into your schedule and your child's. Using inhalers is often a challenge, and you may be concerned that she may not be getting enough of the medicine or too much.

Very often, if symptoms haven't improved, it may simply be that your child is having difficulty using an inhalation device and isn't getting the right amount of prescribed medication in the airways. You should always plan on reviewing the use of inhalation devices in the doctor's office, but it is particularly important if you haven't seen improvement.

Waiting to see if things get better during week two is not, in my view, a good strategy. Your stance, if not that of your child's physician, should be to see immediate change and that you both need to get to the bottom of any issue. I am not suggesting that you and your child will have reached your asthma goals in one week, but you should be observing noticeable changes for the better.

Adhering to the Prescribed Treatment Plan

Your child's symptoms will certainly not improve after the first week if you are using the medications inconsistently or incorrectly. Some parents and children avoid medications because of fears about side effects. As you know from Chapter 4, inhaled corticosteroids are the mainstay of childhood asthma treatment. They are extremely safe when used in appropriate doses, with virtually no side effects. They are more effective than quick-relief medicines, which children are forced to rely on when they aren't taking corticosteroids and which have more side effects. And remember, that the corticosteroids taken for asthma are a completely different compound from the steroids often abused by athletes. There is absolutely no connection between the two. If your child's physician has failed to prescribe an inhaled corticosteroid for airway inflammation, limiting the prescription to albuterol or other quick-acting medication, this also needs to be addressed, as inhaled corticosteroids are strongly recommended in children for all but the mildest of asthma cases.

Check the Timing of Medications

In addition, you may find that you aren't giving your child medicines as you should or that you have inadvertently given them to her at the wrong times. Ideally, inhaled corticosteroids should be taken in the morning (after the peak-flow meter reading) and in the late afternoon. Children with very mild persistent asthma not on corticosteroids may be prescribed a leukotriene modifier, which they can take before bed.

Working parents may find it difficult to give the afternoon dose of corticosteroid. If so, you should tell your physician and help him develop a schedule that fits better with your life, such as having your child take the second dose at dinnertime or, in some cases, giving the after-school counselor or caregiver physician permission to administer the medication.

If the problem lies somewhere with the physician, then you will need to address the issues in the next visit or call. If you feel that the hurried nature of the office visit leaves you no time to ask your questions about treatment, then write them down beforehand. A simple checklist serves as a reminder and time saver. You can ask your questions pointedly, not worry about forgetting, and focus on the answers that you get—all time-efficient approaches to proactively working with your child's physician.

If Parents Disagree About the Asthma Treatment Approach

It may be difficult to deal with a disagreement over whether and how to get treatment for your child. As I discussed in Chapter 5, some people have very strong views about physicians and the use of medications, and may want to try alternatives ranging from nutritional substances to breathing programs to treat a child's asthma. While there is very little data to support such approaches and most children with asthma require medication, it is possible to compromise.

By working with your physician and each agreeing that your child's health is paramount, you can incorporate some alternative methods for one week to see if they help or, at the very least, don't interfere with your child's improvement. If so, then there is no harm in continuing them. However, alternatives minus the use of asthma medications generally don't offer improvement in symptoms, and decisions will need to be made with your spouse if the stalemate continues even in the face of ongoing symptoms. If so, you should insist that your physician refer you to an asthma specialist, as your child will require close monitoring and the guidance of an expert.

Monitoring Symptoms at Home

Monitoring your child's symptoms with a peak-flow meter and recording the results in the asthma management plan (as well as other things you may notice during the week with respect to your child's health) are a powerful tool in proactive asthma care. This tool is a simple way to focus your attention on how your child is doing and is a critical factor in your ability to assess whether there is a problem that needs immediate attention. The traffic light model's Red, Yellow, and Green Zones from Chapter 6 are an easy way for you and your child to keep track of symptom improvement, potential problems, and specifically how your child responds to asthma triggers and allergens—say, with watery eyes, sneezing, or coughing.

The trouble is that, too often, physicians don't encourage the use of peak-flow meters or asthma diaries, and parents are left to too much guesswork. In fact, while the diary and monitoring may seem like a chore at first, this method is far easier than trying to assess your child's symptoms and progress in your head. Using a peak-flow meter and keeping track of symptoms and when they occur with Red, Yellow, and Green Zones help remove the second-guessing and ambiguity that get in the way of reaching symptom freedom. That way, you and your child don't have to remember all the details of the week, but rather you have a written assessment instead.

Securing an Asthma Diary

But what if, even when you ask, the importance of these monitoring tools is downplayed? It may be that, as a pediatrician or family practice physician, your doctor doesn't have asthma diaries to distribute to patients and hasn't had a great deal of experience with patients using peak-flow meters. Some clinicians think patients won't follow through with at-home monitoring, so they don't make a point of encouraging patients to use the diary. If this is the case, go to the website of the American Academy of Allergy, Asthma and Immunology (www.aaaai.org), and download the asthma diary as often as you need to.

Securing a Peak-Flow Meter

For the peak-flow meter, you will need a prescription, so do some quick homework on the Internet to find out about the peak-flow meters that are available (see the Resources section). Then, in week three, you can discuss what you learned with your physician and determine the peak-flow meter that will work best.

This approach may be more proactive than many parents are used to, but stretching beyond your comfort level can be extremely empowering and productive. Moving past any discomfort is a basic cornerstone of proactive asthma care. It is, in short, what *proactive* means, and when exercised, it changes dynamics and situations for the better. You may not be used to questioning a physician or presenting him with information you gleaned from a website. But in truth, your physician is probably used to it. He may find it a bit unsettling and may prefer that patients took all of their cues from him, but his own opinions about how involved parents and patients should be in their own health care is, in all truth, irrelevant.

You, as the parent of a child with asthma, need to become a full partner in your child's health. Asthma is the kind of disease that requires ongoing monitoring and assessment of symptoms by you and your child. Moreover, it demands attention even when she is feeling well. As a highly unpredictable, chronic disease, asthma can never be ignored. You and your child have to work with your physician to gain control over asthma and maintain control into the future. The value of parental involvement in asthma treatment is well documented, and the impact is clear: the more involved parents and children are in their own care, through awareness, monitoring, and education, the better a child feels, and the greater the symptom improvement.

If Your Doctor Does Not Welcome the Proactive Asthma Care Approach

Your physician should welcome your involvement. But if he is less than enthusiastic, that should not deter you or your child from adopting a proactive asthma care stance. You may choose to reconsider your choice of physician, and I will discuss such a decision in Chapter 9. However, for now, you may want to monitor your physician's attitudes as well as your child's symptoms so that you can also assess whether the relationship is one you want to continue.

Addressing Asthma Triggers Within Your Control

Another reason why symptoms may not have improved is failure to address and eliminate asthma triggers, particularly those in the home. Week two is the time to look inward—specifically, to the asthma triggers in the home, school, or day care that increase your child's risk of having an asthma episode. Earlier in the book, I discussed the wide range of asthma triggers, from outdoor air pollution to allergens, such as pollen and cat dander. As parents, you have more control over some triggers than others, and the home environment is, in large part, yours to change.

Identifying the Culprits

An asthma trigger is any substance that irritates your child's airways. Because the airways of children with asthma are inflamed and hypersensitive, any number of irritants and allergens—found outside and inside the home—can irritate the lining of the airways and provoke an asthma episode. It isn't always easy to identify the triggers that prompt asthma symptoms in your child, and isolating and removing the culprits can take some detective work on your part, but avoiding and eliminating triggers will make a big difference in your child's well-being. To simplify the process, we'll review those that cause problems for most children with asthma and that can be quickly remedied.

The most common asthma triggers include:

• **Dust or, more accurately, dust mites:** These microscopic parasites live off of the flakes of human skin that we all shed every day. Unfortunately, most homes, including yours, are host to millions of these creatures. Dust mites can be found on virtually all household surfaces, but they flourish in thick, plushy fibers (particularly those on which we sleep or sit) and in humid environments.

• **Animal dander:** Dander is found in cats, dogs, and other furry pets.

• **Cockroach allergens:** More specifically, it is the dung from the insects that causes problems with asthma.

• **Indoor mold:** Leaky faucets, pipes, humidifiers, vaporizers, sprinklers, and leaky roofs are all prime breeding grounds for mold.

• **Tobacco smoke:** Smoke from cigarettes, cigars, or pipes and smoke-laden clothes are known to provoke asthma symptoms.

• **Wood-burning stoves and fireplaces:** The vast majority of children with asthma simply cannot tolerate the irritating smoke from burning wood, and every effort must be made to reduce your child's exposure to it.

Removing or managing asthma triggers does shift household routines—from how you wash bed linens to removing carpeting in bedrooms—and force decisions that you wish you did not have to make. Those concerning the family pet are often the most difficult, since the best strategy is to remove the pet from the house or at least keep the pet out of the child's room. Creating a trigger-free environment isn't always easy, but the quicker you make the changes, the faster you will see your child's asthma improve.

The Asthma Trigger-Control Shopping List

Parents often delay making important household changes, and I can understand why. Revamping routines and decor, finding a new home for the family cat, and determining whether or not to purchase asthma-control products can be a major project. The checklists that follow should help you through the process.

The childhood asthma epidemic has had one silver lining: the proliferation of products that help control household asthma triggers. There are room air filters, dehumidifiers, vent filters, and covers for pillows and mattresses that are very effective in controlling dust mites, molds, and other indoor allergens. Many can be purchased online, but if you are uncomfortable buying products electronically, you can find them at major department stores and retail chains specializing in personal care equipment. Your health care professional's office staff may also have some ideas about where you can purchase asthma products locally. Here is what you'll need, and why:

- **Allergen-proof encasings for mattresses and box springs:** Dust mites proliferate in linens and soft, plushy surfaces that have been close to human skin for a long time.
- **Allergen-proof encasings for pillows:** Dust mites also love pillows, a particular problem when your child is inhaling them during sleep.
- **Air duct filters:** These items filter out animal dander and other allergens and irritants from your child's room. You can purchase them to cover the air ducts in your child's room; however, the effectiveness of air duct filters has never been proven.
- **Boric acid traps:** If you live in a city, you no doubt have dealt with the unwelcome cockroach problem. The dung from cockroaches is an allergen. Laying boric acid traps can help, but use caution with children because they may think the boric acid is candy.
- **Dehumidifiers:** These products help maintain an indoor humidity of less than 50 percent, hindering the growth of mold and dust mites. Humidifiers also may be necessary during periods of extreme dry or cold weather, which also can provoke asthma symptoms. Ideally, the humidity level should be kept between 20 and 50 percent.

- **Room air filters:** Preferably you want to buy the HEPA-type, which trap fine air particles, including dander and dust mites. Put them in your child's bedroom, which typically has the highest concentration of dust mites and indoor allergens.

Setting Up a Trigger-Free Home

Once you've gathered the products you'll need, it will be time to start making your home more "environmentally friendly" for your child. The following sections can be used as a guide to get your house in asthma order.

Dealing with Dust Mites

You must use your allergen-proof encasings, vacuum them every fourteen days, and wash them every three to six months. The bed linens (sheets and pillowcases) should be washed weekly. A water temperature of 130 degrees is needed to kill dust mites, but the American Academy of Pediatrics recommends that in homes with young children, water temperature be set at no higher than 120 degrees. You will have to increase the water temperature when you're washing her bed linens and then lower it to 120 degrees when finished. You should also replace any feather (down) pillows with polyester or other synthetic and consider removing any carpeting from your child's room and, if possible, from other rooms in the house; eliminating or reducing the number of stuffed toys; removing any humidifiers or vaporizers; and keeping the humidity to less than 50 percent.

Getting Rid of Animal Dander

If you have animal dander from cats, dogs, birds, or other pets with fur or feathers, at minimum, keep the pet out of your child's bedroom and off upholstered furniture and carpets. You should also remove all products made from feathers, such as down comforters and pillows. Some parents attempt to wash pets weekly to remove dander, but according to the data on pet washing, it is ineffective. In addition, as difficult as it may be, you should strongly consider finding the pet a new home.

Smoke from Tobacco, Fireplaces, and Wood-Burning Stoves

Make sure that your child is not exposed to smoke at home or else-where, and forbid any smoking around her or in your house. Also, don't use fireplaces or wood-burning stoves, and ask that they not be used by others when your child is around. If your child is visiting friends, ask ahead whether anyone in the home will be smoking or using wood-burning fireplaces or stoves, and strongly consider ruling out any visits or play dates if the answer is yes (or switch the play date to your home, where you know you can control this trigger).

Getting Rid of Cockroach Allergens

Never leave food or trash uncovered. To exterminate, you can use boric acid traps or a spray insecticide, but keep children out of the house until the smell dissipates.

Avoiding Indoor Mold

To protect your child from indoor mold, fix leaky faucets and pipes and avoid using vaporizers and humidifiers. If you have indoor plants, avoid overwatering or letting water collect at the bottom of the plant or flower pot. The standing water can promote mold growth. You should aim for a home environment that is less than 50 percent humidity to reduce mold and dust mites. You can also place a low-wattage lightbulb in the basement crawl spaces in order to retard mold growth.

Getting "Uncontrollable" Triggers Under Control

Reconfiguring your decor and deciding what to do about your cat are difficult and potentially stressful changes to make, but they are within your control. What do you and your child do about the asthma trig-gers that are uncontrollable? Put simply, you need to do the best you can to anticipate and help her avoid triggers that come from outside the home or that, in the course of daily living, are inevitable. Such triggers include weather changes, viral infections, and environmental irritants, such as smog, pollen in spring and fall, and fumes.

Clearing the Air: Dealing with Weather Changes

Many children with asthma are extremely sensitive to weather changes, particularly increases in humidity or very cold temperatures, and poor air quality, such as smog. While you can't control the weather or air pollution, you should have no problem monitoring weather and air-quality reports. Today's weather forecasts are not only prolific—with nonstop weather channels and attention to the weather on daily local newscasts, online, and through your daily newspapers—but comprehensive. Pay particular attention to changes in humidity, as your child may have an increase in symptoms on very humid days as well as on days that are cold and dry. In addition, damp weather and increased humidity breed dust mites and mold, which can prompt asthma symptoms if your child is allergic to any of them.

Some children experience problems from the weather change itself, so monitoring for "a change in the weather" is important. If the forecast points to changes that can prompt asthma episodes in your child, you can be ready with quick-relief medication or discuss increasing her daily dose of corticosteroid if necessary. In addition, attention to the forecast could also serve as a reminder to keep humidity levels constant in the home by keeping windows closed and using air conditioners on humid days.

Environmental Irritants and Allergens

Just as attention must be paid to weather changes; the same holds true for spring and fall days with moderate to high pollen and mold counts. If your child has been checked for allergies and they were on the list of offenders, then allergy management needs to be a component of your overall asthma management plan. As I discussed earlier, allergies are often overlooked in asthma treatment, even though they are one of the main factors contributing to asthma symptoms in children.

Tree and grass pollen in the spring and early summer, mold in the spring and fall, and weeds in the fall are troublemakers in the majority of children over age five who have asthma, and need to be monitored along with weather. Very often, children need to double the dose of inhaled corticosteroid and increase the use of quick-relief medication when the season changes. These allergens also may require you to change some household habits—including opening windows to fresh spring breezes—that may be a bit difficult to give up but are necessary to help your child avoid symptoms.

For example, if you live in climates with dramatic changes in seasons, such as the Northeast and the Midwest, opening windows and doors on those first spring or fall days may be pleasant but, unfortunately, problematic. Pollen counts are typically highest in the morning or late afternoon. It is important to stem your urge to "let in springtime" by keeping windows and doors shut and running an air conditioner, if necessary, on spring and fall days when pollen is at a peak. Let indoors, pollen will affect household air quality and stick to clothes, upholstery, and linens, causing your child to cough and wheeze even when pollen counts have dropped later in the day. High-pollen days can spark an asthma episode even in children who had control of symptoms all winter long. So it's very important to monitor pollen counts as part of your weather watching, and make sure that you minimize your child's exposure.

It's impossible, in most cases, to totally avoid pollen exposure, but there are some strategies for reducing its impact:

- Keep windows closed. Use air conditioning in your car or home if possible.
- Encourage your child to stay indoors, particularly in the afternoon (when pollen counts may be at their highest levels).
- Make sure she shampoos and showers each night, to wash off the pollen.

In addition, typically, allergy medications—both prescription and over-the-counter antihistamines and/or nasal steroids—can help control inhaled allergies, both indoor and from pollen. However, in some children, the medications are not completely effective. You may find in later weeks that your child's allergies are too severe to be helped by allergy medications or the problem goes beyond seasonal allergies and your child has symptoms year-round (both indoor and outdoor allergies). If faced with a difficult allergy problem, you may want to explore the potential of immunotherapy, or allergy shots, with your physician. A more complete discussion of immunotherapy can be found in Chapter 9.

Keeping Viruses at Bay

There is no way to completely prevent your child from contracting an upper respiratory virus. As the parent of a young child or teenager, you know that children are often the first to bring a virus home from day care, school, or camp. But for children with asthma, upper respiratory viruses, including colds, bronchitis, or the flu, can prompt very severe symptoms. In fact, upper respiratory viral infections are the leading asthma trigger, especially in children under age five, and can often land a young child in the emergency department or hospital.

While it certainly poses a challenge, try to reduce your child's exposure to viruses as much as possible. You must proactively ask parents or caregivers whether children in other homes have colds or coughs and, if so, politely opt out of the play date or party. Keep your home as infection-free as possible. Some data suggest that cleaning surfaces frequently with a disinfectant can kill viruses that cause colds and other infections that can linger on tabletops, doorknobs, countertops, and other surfaces for days and are one of the main routes for illness. There are much stronger data for the benefits of frequent hand washing, which you should encourage in your child and the entire household.

While the day-care debate has swirled in medical circles for years, it remains inconclusive whether children with asthma should avoid day care. Studies do show that children in day care get sicker more often than those who are at home, but that stands to reason. Children exposed to other children or siblings are more apt to contract viruses than those who spend less time with other children. Conversely, there is also evidence to show that very young children (those under age one) exposed to other children in a day-care environment develop an "inner protection" against allergies as they grow and that being in day care may reduce the severity of allergies, even in children with asthma.

Moreover, keeping a child out of day care or any child-care environment may not be possible for a host of valid reasons—from family finances to a parent's emotional well-being. I do not advocate that children with asthma be permanently pulled from a day-care or preschool environment simply because they have asthma. In extreme circumstances—as when a child is continually getting sick and subsequently experiencing severe asthma episodes—it may be necessary to remove a child temporarily until the asthma symptoms are brought under control and her condition has stabilized, as this cycle can land a child in the emergency department or require hospitalization.

However, I do strongly recommend that parents work with day-care center employees and counselors to ensure that your child's risks of getting sick are minimized and that they know what needs to be done in the event of an asthma episode. You will explore how to most effectively work with day-care center workers and other child-care providers in Chapter 8.

In addition to helping your child avoid viruses, you should also ensure that she receives an annual flu shot. Provided they are not allergic to eggs, all children with asthma need a flu shot and are considered a priority during any flu vaccine shortage.

How Your Child Should Feel by the End of Week Two

The week two office visit is the perfect opportunity to build your confidence in how you are managing asthma with your child. You should leave the physician's office feeling assured that you have the information and the tools you need to monitor her progress over the next two weeks. Ideally, any concerns or hesitancy are addressed in the visit, your questions are answered sufficiently, and you feel confident in your child's use of the inhaler or nebulizer and peak-flow meter. More importantly, your sense of being in control and fully participating in the process of helping her gain control of asthma symptoms will be heightened, and you will have gone beyond any feelings of powerlessness. You will have taken the first critical steps in proactive asthma care and begun the essential task of showing her, by example, how to live her life as an empowered asthma patient.

8

Week Three

Improving Life and Symptoms
Away from Home

BY WEEK THREE, you and your child should be experiencing the benefits of proactive asthma care. Symptoms should be noticeably reduced, and your child's peak-flow readings should indicate that breathing is returning to normal. As the parent of a child with asthma, you should have begun to experience the confidence that comes with taking control of his health, forging an active, rather than passive, relationship with his physician, and putting some practical monitoring, medication, and trigger-avoidance strategies into practice at home that, once learned and incorporated, become part of the fabric of daily life. With these important basics in place, it is time to look outside the home to your child's wider world and how it affects his asthma. This chapter will be devoted to helping you set up a school team for your child that is both informed and supportive.

Assembling Your Asthma Team

At your week three office visit, you should enlist the support of your child's physician in developing an asthma management plan for his life away from home: school, after-school, day care, camp, and extracurricular environments. Working with your physician, your plan needs to ensure that he is able to avoid asthma triggers and get help from other adults if he starts experiencing symptoms.

As a proactive parent, you will need to lead this process along with your child. You will be putting a team in place to work together to keep him symptom-free and safe throughout the day. The team will be a critical component of your overall asthma management plan and will contribute to your ability to help him reach his asthma goals. The team members—you, your child's physician, his teachers, school nurse, principal, coaches, after-school and day-care counselors, sitters, and nanny—will be guided by the needs of your child.

For the purposes of this chapter, I will refer in large part to your efforts with teachers, nurses, and other school personnel, but the plan applies to after-school and day-care counselors (and the day-care nurse, if available), coaches, music and dance instructors, babysitters and nannies, relatives and friends, and scout leaders—in fact, any adult in charge of supervising and caring for your child.

In addition, your child needs to take an active role as a team member, particularly since you won't be present at school or camp to help him, should he start experiencing symptoms. As we've discussed, children as young as age eight can be active participants in their own care. They can understand their condition, be made aware of triggers, and learn how and when to take medications and monitor their breathing. Children at this age can also be mindful of asthma myths and stereotypes and be supported in correcting their classmates and even teachers who assume that their asthma has to limit their activities because they are "sick."

If your child is young, he can still begin to understand his asthma and how he can help himself to feel better and cooperate in taking medications. Even the youngest of children are their own best gauge for how they are feeling. Whether it's coughing, chest tightness, or other symptoms, children are in the best position to tell adults around them that they need medication or medical help. But this ability to communicate, to remind a teacher or coach that they need to use an inhaler before exercising or that they are experiencing symptoms, also demands that the adults in their lives are educated about asthma, are aware of potential symptoms, and can respond if medical help is needed. It is also important that teachers and caregivers understand that your child should never be treated differently because of asthma and should not be restricted from activities.

As a pivotal team member, your child will learn to communicate his needs during the school day. He will also gain the self-confidence and awareness he needs to tell his friends and classmates in a matter-of-fact way that he has asthma and that, other than taking precautions to avoid triggers and preventive measures involving exercise, he can do all that they can do. He can explain that symptoms make it hard for him to breathe, and if they hear him coughing or wheezing, he could be having an asthma attack, and they should seek help from a teacher or school nurse. The tools he learns as a member of the school asthma team he will create with you will give him the initial skills he will need to manage asthma socially throughout his life.

Creating an Asthma-Friendly Environment at School

As the school asthma "team leader," you are going to need a game plan to educate and motivate your team members to create and maintain an asthma-friendly environment at school or day care. A positive and energetic approach will go a long way to creating the goodwill and enthusiasm you will want from your school team throughout the year. Your efforts will help not only your child, but no doubt his classmates with asthma.

Setting Up Initial Meetings with Teachers

The game plan should include up-front meetings at the start of the school or day-care year. Ask to meet your child's teacher as well as the school or day-care "asthma champion"—this is usually a person who has been designated by the principal to head up the school's response to asthma. Typically, that person is the school nurse, who makes sure that teachers and other school personnel are familiar with asthma symptoms, knows how to respond to asthma episodes and emergencies, and works to minimize common asthma triggers.

If your child is in day care, meetings should be with a day-care nurse (if there is one), the center director, or the assistant director, as well as your child's day-care counselors. If he is in an after-school program, the program director and his counselors should also be on your meeting lineup.

In addition, you should meet with the directors, coaches, or counselors of his extracurricular sports teams, dance instruction, gymnastics coaches, music instructors, and scout troop leaders, as they most often deal with asthma symptoms in children.

When summer arrives, it will be important for you to meet with camp directors and counselors as well. With your asthma-friendly checklist, your school asthma management plan, and your agenda, you can look forward to an organized and productive session.

Asthma 101: What Teachers Need to Know About Asthma

To ensure that your meetings are productive and thorough, bring some general asthma information and your child's medication inhaler and holding chamber (or nebulizer). Set an agenda, and plan to discuss the following topics:

- General overview of childhood asthma, which you may have received from your physician or downloaded from a credible website, such as the American Academy of Allergy, Asthma and Immunology (www.aaaai.org) or the American College of Allergy, Asthma and Immunology (www.acaai.org)
- Typical triggers and symptoms
- Brief history and some specifics on your child's condition
- Instructions on how to use a peak-flow meter either for routine school-day monitoring or during an asthma episode
- Your child's medication, with a focus on quick-relief medication
- Side effects from your child's medications that may have an impact on school performance
- What to do if your child experiences symptoms or an asthma episode
- Respect for your child's right to privacy and courtesy about having asthma and taking medications (that is, your child is not ready to have his asthma made public or have his need to

take medications be announced or discussed in front of classmates)

- The recognition that the nasal allergies or cough that often accompany asthma are not due to colds or upper respiratory infections and that your child is not contagious to others

You can use the Asthma-Friendly Checklist and the Student Asthma Action Card (Figure 8.1, on pages 132 and 133) at these meetings. Your physician may have copies of a management plan that he can review and complete with you. If he doesn't, you can make copies of the one in Figure 8.1 and take it to the school meeting with you. In fact, it is a good idea to make copies of the checklist and management plan in this book so that you can use them each year for your annual meetings with new teachers and school personnel. The Asthma-Friendly Checklist offers a series of questions that can help you assess your school's "asthma-friendly" quotient, so you know exactly what you are dealing with and can work with school personnel to change the environment, if necessary.

If the answer to any of the checklist questions is no, then your child may be facing challenges and obstacles at school that keep him from

Asthma-Friendly Checklist

How Asthma-Friendly Is Your School?	Yes	No
Is the school tobacco-free all of the time?	——	——
Does the school maintain good indoor air quality? (Does it make every effort to reduce fumes from pesticides, perfumes, cleaning chemicals, paints, and other strong odors?)	——	——
Does the school vacuum daily to remove dust mites?	——	——
Does the school keep furry pets out of the school and classrooms?	——	——
Is a school nurse available all day, every day?	——	——

	Yes	No
If not, is a nurse available to the school to assist students with asthma in following their management plan, managing symptoms, and handling issues with sports, physical education, and field trips?	____	____
Can children take medicine at school as recommended by their physician and parents?	____	____
Can they carry their asthma medication with them?	____	____
Does the school have an emergency plan for taking care of a child having an asthma episode?	____	____
Do school personnel know exactly what to do, who to call, and when to call physicians or the ambulance?	____	____
Does someone (school nurse or other staff member) teach the school staff about asthma, asthma management plans, and asthma medicines?	____	____
Does someone teach all students about asthma and how to help a classmate who has it?	____	____
Do students have good options for fully and safely participating in physical education class and recess?	____	____
Do students have access to medicines before PE class?	____	____
Can they modify exercise or activities when they need to?	____	____

Adapted from American Academy of Allergy, Asthma and Immunology, Inc., "Pediatric Asthma: Promoting Best Practice: Asthma Education Handouts for Healthcare Professionals" (2003). Used by permission.

achieving his asthma goals. As his parent, you need to meet with school personnel and stay committed to rectifying the problem. More important, you need to involve and encourage your child to communicate any concerns or problems during the school day to the school nurse, his teacher, or other school personnel.

The Student Asthma Action Card offers teachers and other personnel a concise overview of your child's asthma triggers, treatments, and emergency plan. You should complete this plan with your physician and your child. If your child is in elementary school, then you will most likely need to have these conversations at the start of the school year. However, as your child moves through middle school and high school, and grows increasingly more comfortable with discussing his asthma, he can be at the forefront, initiating these discussions and letting school personnel know the first week of school that he has asthma and a management plan.

As you've read in previous chapters, asthma can have an impact on your child's emotional and physical well-being, and your meetings should include a discussion of both. Ideally, these meetings should include your child, who can speak directly about his asthma triggers and how he experiences an asthma episode. He can also demonstrate how to use a peak-flow meter and other devices. The meetings need not be long. You can accomplish all you need to in about thirty minutes. Typically, teachers and school nurses find it most convenient to meet before class starts in the morning or after school is dismissed in the afternoon.

By meeting's end, if you have used the completed asthma management plan as a guide, the adults in charge of your child's day should know:

- The early warning signs of an asthma episode in your child
- How to make sure your child gets the quick-relief medication he needs if he experiences symptoms
- When to call you, the physician, or the ambulance
- How to use a peak-flow meter
- How to assess the readings against your child's personal best
- How to help your child use a spacer or holding chamber

Figure 8.1a Student Asthma Action Card

Asthma and Allergy Foundation of America

Student Asthma Action Card

Endorsed by:
National Asthma Education and Prevention Program
EPA

Name:_____ Grade:____ Age:_____

Teacher:_____ Room: _____

Parent/Guardian Name: _____ Ph (H): _____

Address: _____ Ph (W): _____

Parent/Guardian Name: _____ Ph (H): _____

Address: _____ Ph (W): _____

ID Photo

Emergency Phone Contact #1: _____ _____ _____
                              Name   Relationship   Phone

Emergency Phone Contact #2: _____ _____ _____
                              Name   Relationship   Phone

Physician Student Sees for Asthma: _____ Ph: _____

Other Physician: _____ Ph: _____

Emergency Plan

Emergency action is necessary when the student has symptoms such as _____,

_____, _____ or has a peak-flow reading of _____ .

Steps to take during an asthma episode:

1. Check peak flow.
2. Give medications as listed below. Student should respond to treatment in 15-20 minutes.
3. Contact parent/guardian if _____
   _____
4. Recheck peak flow.
5. Seek emergency medical care if the student has any of the following:

✓ Coughs constantly

✓ No improvement 15-20 minutes after initial treatment with medication and a relative cannot be contacted.

✓ Peak flow of _____

✓ Hard time breathing with:
   • Chest and neck are pulled in with breathing
   • Stooped body posture
   • Struggling or gasping

✓ Trouble walking or talking

✓ Stops playing and can't start activity again

✓ Lips or fingernails are gray or blue

IF THIS HAPPENS, GET EMERGENCY HELP NOW!

Emergency Asthma Medications

Name	Amount	When to Use
1. _____	_____	_____
2. _____	_____	_____
3. _____	_____	_____
4. _____	_____	_____

(next page)

Student Asthma Action Card

Reprinted from American Academy of Allergy, Asthma and Immunology, Inc., "Pediatric Asthma: Promoting Best Practice: Asthma Education Handouts for Healthcare Professionals" (2003). Used by permission.

Figure 8.1b Student Asthma Action Card (continued)

Daily Asthma Management Plan

Identify the things that start an asthma episode (check each that applies to the student.)

☐ Exercise   ☐ Strong odors or fumes   ☐ Molds

☐ Respiratory infections   ☐ Chalk dust / dust   ☐ Foods _____

☐ Change in temperature   ☐ Carpets in the room

☐ Other _____

☐ Animals   ☐ Pollens

Comments: _____

Control of School Environment
(List any environmental control measures, pre-medications, and/or dietary restrictions that the student needs to prevent an asthma episode.)

_____
_____
_____
_____

Peak-Flow Monitoring
Personal Best Peak-Flow Number: _____

Monitoring Times: _____ _____ _____ _____

Daily Medication Plan

	Name	Amount	When to Use
1.			
2.			
3.			
4.			

Comments/Special Instructions

_____
_____
_____

For Inhaled Medications

☐ I have instructed (name) _____ in the proper way to use his/her medications. It is my professional opinion that he/she should be allowed to carry and use that medication by him/herself.

☐ It is my professional opinion that

_____ should not carry his/her inhaled medication by him/herself.

_____ _____
Physician Signature   Date

_____ _____
Parent/Guardian Signature   Date

Student Asthma Action Card

An Action Plan for Managing Symptoms at School

While many teachers and counselors know about asthma and have had children with asthma in their care, they don't know about your child and his asthma symptoms and triggers. They may be unaware of how they inadvertently expose a child to asthma triggers. They may allow classmates to bring a pet to school for show-and-tell, visit zoos and farms on field trips, serve cookies with traces of nuts, or fail to realize that some children—perhaps yours—may be extremely sensitive to certain allergens and should not even be seated next to children eating offending foods during lunch. If your child has an allergy to nuts, then the school personnel need to make sure to guard against your child inadvertently eating a cookie or cupcake in class or at lunch with these ingredients. (Ideally, the school nurse or principal should communicate with all parents that foods with peanuts, nuts, or traces of nuts should not be sent to school for birthday celebrations, as children who cannot join in the celebration because of allergies are bound to feel left out.)

Moreover, if your child has been recently diagnosed, you may be unfamiliar with any restrictions the school may impose on access to asthma medication, participation in activities, or use of peak-flow meters. As a proactive parent, your ally is always information, so that you can make informed decisions about your child's well-being.

You already know the value of an asthma management plan. It serves as your record on asthma symptoms, your diary of peak-flow readings, and your gauge on whether your child is moving into a Yellow Zone of caution. You will need a similar asthma plan for school, after school, or day care.

The school-based plan of action is the guide for school nurses, your child's teachers, and the principal on what to do to both guard against an asthma episode (by controlling school asthma triggers, for example) and what steps to take if your child begins to have symptoms. The action plan should not be limited to one person, but should be given to anyone who spends time with your child during the school day: all of his teachers (not only his "primary" and physical education teachers, but his music and art teachers, after-school counselors, coaches, and the teachers who guide clubs and other after-school activities), as well as the school nurse. If your child is in day care or preschool, then the center or preschool director, counselors, and teachers should have a copy of the plan as well.

Like the management plan you use at home, the one for school should be simple and straightforward, with information that school or day-care personnel can quickly assess and act on, if necessary. Specifically, the plan needs to have the following components:

- Up-to-date emergency numbers, including the name and number of your child's physician and backup emergency numbers of friends and nearby relatives should you not be reachable
- A list of your child's asthma triggers, including those found in schools
- A list of your child's typical symptoms
- The names of the quick-relief medications your child uses
- Your child's personal best peak-flow number and monitoring times
- The daily medication plan
- Physician and parent signatures permitting your child to carry his asthma medications with him during the school day (if you and your physician have determined that your child has achieved a level of maturity and responsibility so that he can)
- Steps to take if your child experiences symptoms, including taking a peak-flow reading
- When to call an ambulance

Your child's physician should work with you to develop the plan and help you manage any of the challenges that are bound to arise in building your school asthma team. But as a proactive parent, you may need to lead the process, alerting your physician to your concerns and questions about managing asthma outside the home and building a solid and educated team of asthma-fighting allies.

Monitoring and Medications

Your child should be taking his long-acting controller medication outside of the typical school day—in the morning before leaving for school and late afternoon. Quick-relief medication should be available whenever your child needs it, and particularly before physical education class or sports activities. While much has changed with respect to access to medications, there are still school districts that prohibit children from carrying their medication with them during the school day.

You should respectfully challenge that restriction if it still exists in your district, and explain the importance of permitting children to carry quick-relief medication for both emotional and physical reasons if your physician had given the go-ahead. Remember, children often feel embarrassed early on about their asthma, which can lead to non-adherence with their treatment. Since reducing embarrassment is important, it is generally preferable for children to be able to carry inhalers and use them in an administrative office or empty classroom with some degree of privacy. Needing to ask permission to go to the nurse or principal's office prior to physical education or recess is another impediment to adherence, as it makes children feel different and stand out. In many cases, schools will agree to allow children to self-carry if they receive a physician's note. But not always.

If you find yourself fighting an uphill battle or realize that changing school policy may take some time, then at a minimum, insist that your child have easy access to his inhaler at the nurse's office or classroom (he should know where his inhaler is kept). In any case, don't stop working to get rid of policies that separate children from their medication during school. At the same time, bear in mind that your child may lose or misplace his inhaler if he does self-carry, so if possible, make sure that the school nurse or teacher has a spare inhaler.

Day-care workers and directors also need to know how to use a nebulizer, if your child is an infant or toddler. School and day-care personnel should also know or learn how to use a peak-flow meter.

Ideally, a school nurse or other health personnel would be able to take a peak-flow reading in the event your child was experiencing symptoms, giving them a more precise gauge beyond simply observing the extent and severity of symptoms. However, even without a peak-flow reading, your school asthma team members should grasp the basics: that an asthma episode is worsening if symptoms worsen—if an infrequent cough becomes persistent, chest pain continues, and wheezing becomes louder. They should be told that symptoms can progress slowly or quickly, and that there is no way to predict. The teacher, school nurse, or other school or day-care personnel should stay with your child and be prepared to call a physician or ambulance if necessary. The message should be loud and clear: *Asthma symptoms at school or day care demand attention and vigilance from your team.*

You, on the other hand, should leave with a very good sense of your school's experience with asthma, the triggers that can prompt symptoms in your child, and the accessibility your child will have to his quick-relief medication. Run through your Asthma-Friendly Checklist to determine how much action you will need to take to make sure that your child reaches his symptom-free goals.

Controlling Common School and Day-Care Asthma Triggers

As discussed in Chapter 7, common asthma triggers include:

- Dust mites
- Furry animals as classroom pets
- Mold
- Chalk dust
- Carpeting in classrooms
- Strong odors (paint or chemical fumes, perfumes, cleaners)
- Lawn mowing
- Heating and air-conditioning systems (if they haven't been properly cleaned)
- Respiratory viruses
- Cold air
- Exercise

At first, it may seem that you and your child have little control over many of these triggers, but that is where proactive asthma care comes into play. You will need to inform your school team about the problem these substances pose for children with asthma, and take steps to minimize their impact.

As with the home environment, some asthma triggers are more easily reckoned with than others. Making a decision to keep furry pets out of the classroom or distributing to all parents information about permissible and nonpermissible birthday treats via notes in children's backpack folders can be done with relative ease. Your child's teacher can promise not to wear perfume or reduce the use of chalk, and she can direct your child to indoor activities on high-pollen days.

However, the problem of dust mites and mold, for example, may be out of the teacher's control. In these situations, use the skills you've already developed in managing triggers at home. Some you know you can't readily or completely control—such as pollen and outdoor air pollution—but you do what you can to reduce their impact. For example, insist that your child be directed to indoor activities during recess on days with high pollen counts. As most schools—particularly those in humid climates—are havens for dust mites and mold, ask if the teacher can turn on a dehumidifier and/or an air filter when she leaves the classroom at the end of her day. I have never heard of a teacher or school turning down this request, provided, of course, that you, the parent, purchase the product and maintain it.

One great way to minimize the expense and also build a supportive asthma network is to ask permission from the principal to distribute a friendly notice in children's backpacks asking whether other parents of asthmatic children would be interested in contributing to the purchase of a filter, maintaining it, and collaborating to ensure that the school be as trigger-free as possible.

Physical Education Follow-Up

As for asthma symptoms induced by exercise or running or playing hard, you and your child will have to inform teachers and coaches that these symptoms should not exclude your child from activities, but that he may need to use his quick-relief inhaler prior to gym class or sports. I recommend a slightly longer meeting with physical education teachers, coaches and camp counselors, and others who will supervise your child during exercise, as you will need to outline the precautions and preventive measures that your child may need to take with respect to sports activities.

In addition to receiving a copy of the school asthma management plan during your meeting with them, physical education teachers and coaches should get written instructions from you (which you have developed with the help of your child's physician) on special issues with respect to exercise-induced asthma.

Virtually all children with asthma are prone to symptoms during exercise, and some physical education teachers and coaches recognize that fact. It is important that you emphasize that your child should participate fully in all activities without restrictions, provided his asthma symptoms are under control. Still, your child—and most children with asthma—will need to take quick-relief medication prior to exercise, and physical education teachers and coaches should be made aware of this. They also need to know what to do if he does begin to experience symptoms. Your special instructions, which should be drafted with your physician, should include a brief overview of exercise-induced asthma and the medication your child will use to prevent it prior to activity.

Most children with asthma need a five-minute warm-up period and quick-relief medication to minimize the potential for exercise-induced symptoms. By starting the exercise process, your child's airways begin to release the mediators that produce asthma symptoms. Using quick-relief medication stops the process, and symptoms should not resurface throughout the exercise period. This way, he can avoid symptoms for at least a couple of hours of strenuous activity.

Still, even with this effective precaution, physical education can be challenging terrain for your child. Physical education teachers and coaches, in particular, need to be made aware of any sensitivities your child may have regarding sports activities, as they can inadvertently embarrass him with an insensitive comment or label, be overly cautious, or conversely, be too cavalier—failing to recognize that he may be having difficulty after running for long periods or playing strenuously in cold air or on windy days. You may need to tell them that high-pollen or high-smog days may require that physical education class be held indoors. You can gently remind the PE teacher that gym class can sometimes be tricky for children with asthma, and that with his support and encouragement, your child can realize his full potential.

When You Should Keep Your Child Home

Parents are understandably anxious when their child with asthma seems to be coming down with a cold. Sometimes it is hard to tell if he is merely congested; having only minor, easily controlled symptoms;

or if some mild wheezing is going to develop into something worse. A peak-flow reading is your essential first step to knowing where you stand and whether it might be a good idea to keep him home from school. If the peak-flow reading is at 70 percent or lower from his personal best, you may decide that he should not go to school, and certainly if it remains at this level after quick-relief medication. A level this low indicates that he needs his management plan to be adjusted, and you should call his physician.

There are other reasons why he should stay home, which may be signs of uncontrolled symptoms or the onset of an upper respiratory virus that would make him more vulnerable to an asthma episode (along with simply not feeling well). They include:

- Sore throat, swollen neck glands
- Fever of 100 degrees or feeling hot, flushed, and achy
- Wheezing and coughing one hour after taking quick-relief medication
- Weakness or tiredness
- Difficulty breathing or breathing hard and fast

There are also times when you can probably safely send your child to school, provided he has access to his quick-relief inhaler and the school has an up-to-date Student Asthma Action Card. These include:

- Stuffy nose but no wheezing
- Slight wheezing that stops after taking quick-relief medication
- Peak-flow reading of 70 percent or greater after quick-relief medication
- Energy to do normal daily activities
- Ability to breathe without any extra effort

A Day in the Life: Addressing Asthma Stereotypes at School

In a perfect world, the school experience for children with asthma would be no different than for children without. Since children with well-controlled asthma can participate in all school activities without restriction, any problems with school—whether academic or social—

would have nothing to do with asthma. Unfortunately, this scenario is typically not the case for most children. Given the stereotypes and misinformation that still exist about children with asthma, combined with a lack of knowledge about the disease, your child could find himself in any number of embarrassing situations where he is made to feel different. Despite the progress that we have made in understanding and treating childhood asthma, children with the disease are often treated as they were in the 1950s—as different, "sickly," and unable to do all that other children can do. They may become overly identified as the "asthmatic kid" and may be sidelined from sports activities for fear they won't be able to measure up. Conversely, you may find that some teachers or coaches downplay asthma and need to learn that it is a chronic and complicated condition with serious consequences.

Children themselves, who have been frightened by asthma episodes, may be hesitant to join in sports and other activities for fear that they will experience the shortness of breath that found them being rushed to the physician's office or emergency department. To make matters worse, school regulations may forbid them from carrying their inhalers with them during the school day, forcing them to visit the school nurse before physical education and increasing their feelings of being different. Teachers may be oblivious to the asthma triggers that are in the classroom or forget to remove them.

This combination of lack of awareness, stereotyping, fear, assumptions, and an unfriendly asthma environment poses both emotional and physical challenges to children. They may not want to go to school or, when there, may opt out of activities for fear of an asthma episode. Studies have shown that children with asthma are vulnerable to embarrassment and depression throughout their school-age years, often resulting from the knowledge that they have a chronic disease, are "different" from other children, and could have another asthma episode. In fact, recent data found that nearly half of all preteens and teenagers with asthma routinely feel depressed, nervous, and "uptight." Many are angry and uncomfortable primarily because their daily life experience is one of being "different" from their peers.

Watching Out for Signs of Depression

No child wants to feel different from their friends and classmates, and often our efforts to console our children with words of support or counsel—saying, "you're no different from anyone else" and reminding them that millions of children and teens have asthma (most likely several of their classmates and friends or cousins)—fall on deaf ears. Even when symptoms are controlled, children may still experience this feeling of difference. It is not a problem that can be immediately remedied with a couple of conversations and reassurances.

As a parent, you will need to be on the alert for any symptoms of depression in your children throughout adolescence and make sure that your child's physician pays attention to his emotional state as well. If necessary, you should discuss a referral to a counselor or child psychologist. This is crucial not only because your child's emotional well-being is as important as his physical health, but also because we know that children who are depressed or angry about their asthma are less likely to adhere to their treatment plan.

Involving Your Child in His Own Care

This becomes particularly problematic in adolescence, when teens are extremely conscious of fitting in and conforming to their peer group. While there is no surefire solution to avoiding depression or anger in your asthmatic child, I have found that involving children in their care and as an active participant in changing worn-out notions among peers and teachers can make a huge difference in how your child feels about having asthma and managing it at school and elsewhere.

Proactive asthma care is designed in large part to help you create an example for your child of being an empowered patient—a patient who not only is informed about his illness, but also has the inner confidence to talk about asthma and educate fellow students, teachers, and friends about its myths and realities. I have encouraged patients to use this action-based approach to managing asthma in their child's world and have seen it transform asthmatic children from embarrassed and overwhelmed "victims" into more assured—and more cooperative—patients. In Chapter 9, I talk in depth about the rewards of raising an empowered patient. But initially, talking openly about asthma can help alleviate some of the embarrassment and negative emotions that children often struggle with and put asthma in its proper place—as a disease that requires monitoring and attention but need not be the source of embarrassment or humiliation.

As you serve as the head of your child's asthma team, your proactive meetings with the other adults in his life will help communicate this powerful message in matter-of-fact actions and words. In addition to the emotional and social challenges of asthma, your child also confronts a host of allergens and irritants commonly found in schools and day-care environments.

The School's Asthma Report Card: Checking Up on Progress

What if your child's school flunks? If teachers permit pets in the classroom? Or the old, drafty building is home to dust mites and mold? What if children are not permitted to carry inhalers with them during the school day? Or the clarinet teacher has never taught a child with asthma and is too fearful, thinking it best that your child forgo music lessons altogether? What if, unfortunately, your school or day care does not employ a nurse?

It may be easy to get discouraged with the school's failing asthma grade or the overreactions of some adults unfamiliar with asthma, but a proactive approach will help you manage these obstacles and overcome them. First, remember that you need the support of your child's school asthma team, so it's important to work with them as allies, rather than adversaries.

In my experience, teachers, day-care center directors, coaches, and music teachers are open to learning about childhood asthma, helping your child, and changing the environment, if possible. They recognize the responsibility they have to keep your child safe, and they want the tools and information they need to do that. Together, you can address the obstacles that compromise your child's health during the school day.

The team is stronger with the support of a health professional—such as a school nurse or day-care nurse—but nonhealth personnel are perfectly capable of learning about asthma and what to do to minimize triggers and manage symptoms. If you encounter resistance, enlist the support of your child's physician to write a letter or make a telephone call insisting that changes be made.

Week three can be especially busy for a proactive parent and child, but the effort is essential and, to a large degree, satisfying. By enlisting the support of all those in your child's world and encouraging greater awareness and sensitivity, you are building a network of support for your child and a framework that he can use to cultivate his own foundation of support as he grows.

Asthma on the Road

With asthma symptoms under control, it can be easy to forget that your child has a chronic disease that is highly unpredictable, requiring ongoing monitoring and some medication to maintain symptom control. As you no doubt have learned, routines supported by your asthma and school management plans are valuable tools in simplifying the day-to-day care of your child with asthma. Children, and most adults, respond well to routines that keep them on track with monitoring, medication, and trigger avoidance. It is not surprising to find that problems arise when children and parents break from routines.

Even the most careful parents can forget medications or inhaling devices when traveling, or presume that because symptoms are controlled, it is OK to skip medications for a few days. I often get frantic calls when children begin to experience symptoms while visiting far-off relatives or while on vacations. Invariably, the family left the medicines and the nebulizer or inhaler at home. Because this problem is so common, I often recommend parents obtain extra medication before leaving for a trip or before a child leaves for camp. This typically requires your physician to write a note to the insurance company or pharmacist explaining the need for the request.

You should do some homework before you leave and make adjustments to your plans while still at home. If, for example, you aren't satisfied that your initial hotel selection will be clean enough to keep your child symptom-free, it is far easier to change your selection and make a reservation elsewhere before you leave. The same holds true for private homes. If friends have a cat or they smoke and your child is allergic to cat dander or smoke, you may need to stay at a nearby hotel.

Once on the road, keep to the routine you've established. Give medications in the car or plane, keeping to your schedule as much as possible. If your child has food allergies, check menus and ask whether you can speak to the chef before being seated to make sure there will

Travel Checklist: Before You Leave

Preparing for a trip or getting a child ready for camp is decidedly hectic, but a few simple tips can ensure that she stays healthy while traveling:

- Find out if anyone smokes at the home you will be visiting.
- Ask if there are pets.
- Ask whether the pillows or bedding are made of down or feathers, which produce symptoms.
- Check on the weather or air quality of your destination city.
- Reserve a smoke-free room on a nonsmoking floor of hotels and motels.
- Pack your child's inhaler, nebulizer, medications, peak-flow meter, and pillow cover in carry-on luggage. (Battery-powered, portable nebulizers can run off the car battery; and if you don't have a battery-powered nebulizer, you will need to rent one.)
- Pack the asthma management plan.
- Call your child's physician to ask for a recommendation on health care facilities, hospitals, and physicians in areas you will be visiting.
- Determine whether you will need a prescription for medication prior to leaving (to make sure you have enough to last throughout your trip).
- Make sure you take enough medicine with you for the trip, and don't put medication in checked baggage. Always have it with you in your carry-on bags.

be foods your child can eat. Do the same at a friend's house. If food is being served that could provoke symptoms, offer to cook for your child separately and have options on hand if treats with food allergens are served. And remember that changes in routine and increased activities and excitement also can produce symptoms, so balance his activities, making sure that he has time in his day for relaxation and quieter activities.

It does require a bit more focus and diligence, as it is human nature to let things slide while vacationing, but asthma treatment and trigger avoidance should not be one these things.

Asthma Overnighters: Tips for Sleepaway Camps and Sleepovers

While I strongly believe that children with asthma should never be made to feel as though they are "different" from other children, we can't ignore the fact that they do have special concerns that other children don't have. They have to take medication every day, even if they are symptom-free, and they need to prepare for the possibility of symptoms getting worse, even though it is less likely to happen when their asthma is controlled. As I mentioned earlier, children do better when all of the important adults in their world—including camp directors and counselors—are aware, educated members of their asthma management team.

While it is not essential that health care professionals, such as school and day-care nurses, be on the team, it is certainly preferable. For obvious reasons, a nurse will have a greater fluency in medical terminology and processes, which can be helpful in emergencies. She may be alert to your child's overall well-being, more aware of changes in his energy level and symptoms, and more focused on making sure that he takes medication on time, as prescribed. Many parents of children with asthma—in fact, the majority of parents of day-care and school-age children—feel more assured when there is a full-time nurse on staff.

Considering Asthma Camps

For all of these reasons, many parents of children with asthma, particularly those with moderate to severe cases, send their kids to asthma camps each summer. There are an estimated one hundred camps throughout the country, many run by the American Lung Association and the Asthma and Allergy Foundation of America. For some parents, they offer reassurance that camp will be medically supervised and that all of their child's fellow campers will have the same life experience as she does. Children with more serious cases of asthma tend to enjoy asthma camps a great deal, in large part because they provide all of the enjoyment of camp without the anxiety. As we know, children with asthma can often struggle with a lack of self-esteem or negative feelings about having asthma and being different. Even if their asthma is well controlled, they can still harbor anxiety that a sports or social activity will provoke asthma symptoms, which can make camp—particularly a sleepaway camp—a stressful event. Asthma camps can relieve these anxieties altogether.

Considering Other Day and Sleepaway Camps

That said, many children with asthma are uncomfortable with the idea of asthma camp, preferring to be at camps that they feel do not single out children with the disease. Children who can't or won't attend an asthma camp for whatever reason can still enjoy a satisfying camp experience. As with travel, you will need to plan and pack carefully, while also asking some pointed questions to determine the best camp possible for your child that meets your scheduling and financial criteria and your child's interests.

Questions to consider when selecting a camp include:

- Is there a physician or nurse on staff at all times (especially important for overnight camps)?
- Does the camp permit smoking (by staff, for instance) anywhere on the premises?
- What are the living conditions, such as cabins or tents, that may require a change in your child's medication regimen?
- What are the weather conditions?
- What are the nearby medical facilities and hospitals?
- What are the rules for taking medicines?
- Are there animals or pets?
- Are provisions made for children with food allergies?
- Is there easy access to daily medication?

You should also ask the camp director whether children with asthma have attended, and attempt to get a sense of their overall experiences with asthmatic children. If you have the slightest sense that the camp's experience with asthma is limited and that the rigors of the camp would leave little room for accommodating your child's health needs, then move on. It is fine to select a sports-oriented camp, but remember that your child will need to balance intense activities with restful periods that may feature reading or crafts. Make sure that the camp you select makes both you and him feel at ease—physically and emotionally—and assured that he will be in good hands.

What to Pack

Just as when flying, make sure that you pack your child's medicines and devices where he can get at them as needed—such as in his backpack rather than with bus luggage or in the trunk of a car. Here's a handy checklist to make sure you have packed the important items for his asthma care:

- All medicines and devices (inhalers and peak-flow meters)
- Extra prescriptions, to ensure he has enough medication at all times (or extra medication, obtained by asking your child's physician to write a note to the insurance company or pharmacist)
- Your child's asthma action card and management plan
- List of food allergies for camp food personnel
- E-mail addresses, phone numbers, and cell phone numbers for physicians
- A pillow and mattress cover
- All health insurance forms and identification numbers
- Any special written instructions from your child's physician

What to Do When You Get There

As a proactive parent, you may have already discussed your child's asthma needs via telephone with the camp medical personnel, but you should reiterate your instructions when you arrive. The first day of camp is typically quite hectic, with parents and children arriving at once, so you may find that you will need to telephone the next day to make sure that you've covered all of the important points regarding his camp stay.

It is important that your child be a part of the discussions with his camp counselors, whether or not he is attending an asthma camp. Involving your child in the process of educating others about his asthma will make it easier for him to talk about it with his friends. It should also help him deal with any fears he may have about participating in strenuous camp activities or any fatigue or symptoms he may experience while he is there. More importantly, the experience of seeing you in action as a proactive parent and paving the way together helps him build his own repertoire of assertive and proactive behavior in managing his asthma through camp and beyond.

Tips for Sleepovers

Similar to camp, sleepovers demand that you tell other parents or caregivers that your child has asthma and that you therefore need to ask some questions to make sure there aren't things in their environment that could cause symptoms. As with camp, you should:

- Ask about pets and smoking
- Ask about the use of fireplaces or wood-burning stoves
- Find out if the family has been doing renovations or painting (as fumes or particles can have an effect on indoor air quality) or if construction work is being done in the neighborhood

Don't hesitate to opt out gracefully if the environment sounds like it could pose problems. If the problem is temporary—construction or a renovation, for example—then you can plan for future sleepovers. If the problem is ongoing, such as smoking or a cat, then explain that sleepovers would not be possible, and consider having your child's friend for sleepovers at your house.

If the sleepover is a go, then take a page from your school asthma team playbook. You will need to discuss your child's asthma with the other parent and review the asthma management plan with her. It is a good idea to involve the children in the discussion, so that everyone is aware. Keep the discussion matter-of-fact and upbeat. Explain that his medication will make symptoms unlikely, but it is always a good idea to be prepared. It is fine to leave the peak-flow meter at home. Most children with asthma feel uncomfortable with the notion of monitoring asthma at another's home, and that is understandable.

The idea is not to alarm or dramatize, but being proactive means, in large part, anticipating what could happen and planning ahead. Your tone and approach should convey a confidence that your child in all likelihood will be fine. But given that you are not completely in charge of the travel, camp, school, and sleepover environments, there is a greater potential for an asthma episode. Communicating, educating others, and giving them simple tools and the support they need to help your child are, in fact, the antidotes to alarm and anxiety. They help you rest easier when your child is away from home.

9

Week Four

Living (Well) with Asthma and Looking to the Future

WEEK FOUR IS both a turning point and a decision point for parents. If you've followed the steps in the four-week proactive program—combining environmental controls, trigger avoidance, long-acting control medication, and daily peak-flow monitoring—your child should be virtually symptom-free. To assess whether she has reached her asthma goals, check to see whether she has achieved the following benchmarks:

- No symptoms (or very minimal symptoms) day or night
- No asthma episodes
- No activity restrictions
- Near-normal lung function
- Infrequent use of quick-relief medication (only prior to exercise)
- No medication side effects

Your weekly office visits should have built a strong partnership with your child's physician and staff, and your collaboration with school and day-care personnel should have created more asthma-friendly environments outside the home.

If your child has reached her goals, then your physician will most likely maintain the asthma management plan you established in week one for the next three to six months. At the end of three to six months, assuming that your child has remained symptom-free, medication can be reduced. Moving forward, your physician may consider decreasing the dose of inhaled corticosteroids by 25 percent every three months, presuming that you:

- Continue to monitor her breathing
- Contact the physician if she begins experiencing symptoms again
- Contact the physician if her lung function deteriorates

Recent studies tell us that children with mild intermittent asthma can maintain control of symptoms without daily use of inhaled corticosteroids. However, during an asthma exacerbation, they may require medication for a period of time. My goal in asthma therapy has always been to achieve freedom from symptoms and to normalize breathing tests at the lowest possible dose of medication.

But what if your child has not reached her asthma goals at week four? Several factors could be at work, requiring that you review the steps you've taken (or haven't taken) in the first three weeks. As discussed in Chapter 7, you may have not been following the treatment plan as prescribed or following through on environmental controls. Your child may have not been prescribed enough medication in the first few weeks to get her symptoms under control.

Early on, I explained the importance of aggressively treating asthma during the initial four-week period following diagnosis, with the ultimate goal of reducing therapy to the lowest possible dose after three to six months or so. If your child wasn't prescribed a sufficient dose of inhaled corticosteroids, then the airway inflammation precipitating an asthma episode might not have been addressed. She therefore may have continued to rely too heavily on quick-relief medication to stop her symptoms, without taking corticosteroids each day to maintain ongoing symptom control. In addition, there may be asthma triggers at school or day care that still demand attention and, if possible, removal. She may have had an upper respiratory tract infection during that time or untreated allergic rhinitis or sinusitis.

Hopefully, you've retraced your steps over the past three weeks and taken steps to fill any asthma gaps with help from your child's physician, school nurse, day-care center, or other environment. If so, then you may choose to extend the four-week program by two weeks or so, and assess her progress at that point. However, if you get to week six and your child is still far short of a symptom-free life, then you may need to have a hard look at the overall quality of care she has been receiving.

Quality of Care: Should You Change Physicians?

In my practice, I see hundreds of children each year who have been following the treatment plan and whose parents and schools have implemented asthma-trigger controls, yet they are still plagued with persistent symptoms.

Very often, the problem has nothing to do with parent or child. Rather, there may another underlying condition that has not been diagnosed or properly treated by the physician, inadequate or ineffective combinations of medications, or quite frankly, a "bad connection" between the parents and the doctor. The simple fact is that no child should have anything but the mildest of asthma symptoms at week four. Even in children with moderate to severe cases, an effective plan will significantly reduce symptoms from their level when asthma was first diagnosed.

If you've communicated your concern about not meeting your child's asthma goals, and if you feel that your concerns are falling on deaf ears or not being addressed, then you have an important decision to make. You may need to see an asthma specialist or find another pediatrician or family physician.

It can be a difficult and potentially awkward situation, but it is often unavoidable in the treatment of childhood asthma. As I discussed earlier, the current health care system often leaves the treatment of a highly complicated disease in the hands of nonspecialists. I am not at all suggesting that your pediatrician or family practice physician is not a good, caring physician. However, I am saying that he or she is not a specialist in the treatment of asthma and allergy in children. Perhaps subtle and difficult-to-uncover clues are in the way of your child and symptom freedom.

If you decide to change physicians, you will need to do some investigating and interviewing to choose a physician who has the skills, sensitivity, and desire to partner with patients. Some physicians are more attuned to this dynamic than others and are more comfortable working closely with parents and children to improve asthma care and reach asthma treatment goals.

While it is preferable to have that care delivered by an asthma specialist, I realize that it may not be possible. It is also not essential. Many pediatricians and family physicians are well versed in asthma care and committed to collaborating with parents and children. How can you be reasonably assured that your new physician will have these attributes? The following list of questions can help you ascertain whether a physician is a good candidate for your asthma management team:

- Do you have an interest in managing children with asthma?
- Do you have asthma, or do any members of your family?
- Do you have an expertise in the treatment of childhood asthma? Have you taken any special courses or read the current literature?
- Do you set aside times during the week for asthma patients?
- What is your philosophy, that is, your concept of allergy treatment in asthma, asthma prevention, and so forth?
- Are you familiar with how to use an inhaler, peak-flow meter, and asthma management plan?
- Do you have experience working with schools to support adherence to medication and environmental controls?
- Is there anyone on your staff to assist patients in learning how to teach children and parents how to better manage asthma?

If you decide at this point to hold off changing physicians, there are several possible stumbling blocks that, once removed, will find your child on the clear path to a symptom-free life.

Giving Allergies a Shot: Immunotherapy

As you will recall from Chapter 2, more than 90 percent of all children with asthma have allergies. If the allergies are insufficiently treated, the asthma symptoms will not go away, even if the child is being treated with an inhaled corticosteroid or other long-acting medications. Even if she has been taking antihistamine, nasal steroids, or decongestants, they don't work for every child and may be inadequate. It may be time to consider "allergy shots."

If your child is faced with a difficult case of allergies, discuss immunotherapy with her physician. *Immunotherapy*, which is highly effective in controlling allergies, is the medical term for allergy shots. Immunotherapy works similarly to vaccinations. It is typically given to children age five and over with allergic rhinitis, such as upper respiratory allergy that produces sneezing, runny nose, congestion, nasal itching, and watery eyes due to pollen, animal dander, and/or dust mites. (I have treated younger children; however, immunotherapy is difficult to administer in younger children, as they find it hard to cooperate when getting shots.) Immunotherapy isn't recommended for children with food allergies, because it is not effective and can be dangerous.

As with vaccinations, she would receive, through an injection, minute amounts of the allergens that are causing allergic responses. Over time, the immune system becomes less sensitive to the allergen and no longer goes into the "overdrive" response. Immunotherapy not only can relieve symptoms but also can prevent them from returning, even after she has completed the course of treatment.

Injections can be difficult for most children, and they may be averse to undergoing a course of treatment, but the results from immunotherapy are most times worth the discomfort. Every parent of a child with allergies should consider immunotherapy if allergies are severe or aren't well controlled by medication. It is also a good idea if your child has difficulty taking allergy medication or is uncooperative, or if you and she continually forget to take it. Recent studies suggest that administering allergy injections in children with nasal allergy may prevent the development of asthma.

Who Gives Allergy Shots?

Immunotherapy (allergy shots) must be administered under the direction of an allergy specialist. Ideally, it should be given in an allergist's office. If, for reasons of convenience, distance, or cost, treatment by a specialist is not possible, then your pediatrician or family physician can administer the shots, provided the allergist or asthma specialist has given comprehensive instructions. Allergy shots should never be administered without a physician being present.

Time Commitment Involved

Immunotherapy is not accomplished in a single visit. The entire process could take as long as twelve to eighteen months to be effective. It also does not rule out the need for allergy medication and environmental controls. Since immunotherapy takes time to work, your child will need to be taking allergy medicines in the early stages of the process. Environmental controls should be maintained as well. Later on, a successful course of immunotherapy should make it possible to reduce or eliminate the need for allergy medications.

It's also important to note that immunotherapy does require a significant time commitment. You and your child will need to make room in your schedules for the treatment, which is administered in two phases. The first, the buildup phase, involves injections one to two times per week, during which time your child will receive increasing amounts of the offending allergens. The buildup phase, which generally lasts for about six months, is then followed by a maintenance phase, during which she will continue to receive the same dose once every two to four weeks. If the process has been successful, then maintenance treatment should continue for about three to five years.

What to Expect During Treatment

Immunotherapy can be uncomfortable. As a parent, you no doubt have dreaded vaccines but recognize them as necessary. Immunotherapy is delivered with a much thinner and shorter needle than vaccines and is less uncomfortable. You may find that your child is less frightened by the procedure than you had anticipated. Also, like vaccines, it is over quickly, and even the most resistant child can be consoled and supported throughout the visit.

Your child may experience some mild side effects. When administered properly and under a specialist's supervision, immunotherapy is very safe, but occasionally there is some mild itching or swelling at the injection site, which may happen immediately or after several hours and eventually disappears. In very rare instances, she may experience increased allergy symptoms, such as wheezing, sneezing, or hives, which can be managed with epinephrine. Serious reactions are extremely rare, and in the unlikely event that they do occur, physicians are trained in how to treat them. Most reactions to allergy shots occur within twenty minutes after shots are given, so you will need to stay in the doctor's office for at least twenty minutes.

If Treatment Doesn't Work

In some cases, immunotherapy fails to work. If your child doesn't improve after twelve to eighteen months of therapy, then you need to do some detective work with your physician or specialist. It could be that the dose of allergen she received was too low to build immunity, or perhaps not all allergens were identified during allergy testing (for example, she may be getting treatment for animal dander but not receiving a vaccine for tree pollen). If environmental controls at home or school—or nonallergic triggers, such as tobacco smoke—remain a problem, then they could be interfering with her improvement as well. In rare cases, neither physicians nor parents are able to pinpoint the reason that immunotherapy isn't working.

If you've given the process ample time to work, then immunotherapy should be stopped. You may never know why, and you will have to do your best to control all environmental triggers and take careful steps to minimize your child's exposure to dust mites, dander, pollen, and other allergens that may be keeping her from her symptom-free goals.

Checking for Other Undiagnosed Conditions

In addition to beginning immunotherapy, you should also review with your physician the other diseases that can accompany asthma, such as gastroesophageal reflux disease (GERD), sinusitis, and food allergies. If any have been overlooked, they will contribute to asthma symptoms and keep your child from getting better.

When allergies or other asthma-related conditions are diagnosed and properly treated, the turnaround is dramatic. Children struggling with symptoms can feel noticeably better within a few weeks' time when their allergies are tamed. In addition, their need for high doses of asthma medication is reduced, and their well-being and quality of life—and their family's—is restored.

Raising an Empowered Patient

If you have followed the four-week proactive asthma plan, you have given your child not one, but two, very important gifts. The first, of course, is the promise of a childhood with virtually no asthma symptoms. The second, perhaps less obvious, is the gift of learning how to be an empowered patient. Now, I recognize that the word *empowerment* has been somewhat overused, particularly in the realm of mental and physical well-being, but when it comes to managing asthma, empowerment is real and valuable. Studies have repeatedly shown that active and ongoing patient involvement makes a difference in the overall outcome of asthma.

We know from the four-week plan that making a commitment to become proactive and implementing the practical tools needed to put that commitment into action can take a child who was suffering with frequent or uncontrolled symptoms and turn the situation completely around. This, for me, is the true measure of empowerment. It isn't merely a word, but rather, an *activity*, a new way of dealing with and relating to the life circumstance of having a child with asthma. It takes you and your child out of the confusing and overwhelming position of being victimized by asthma and totally dependent on the medical community. It brings both of you to a place where you can begin to take steps that will affect real change—in how you both feel about asthma, how she sees herself, and how you relate to others and the world around you.

From this place of empowerment, you can participate actively in partnerships with your physician and others. You can lead the process of change, giving them the information and tools they need to help you and your child make this happen. Your physician, your child's school and day care, and all of the people in her life are then able to do a much better job of caring for her well-being. The vast majority of people who embrace this proactive posture find it reassuring and rewarding.

As a physician, I am always pleased with the impact that it inevitably has on a patient's outlook, how they feel about themselves, how they internalize having a chronic illness, and ultimately how they improve. I am encouraged by the impact that proactive asthma care has on children. Parents are often surprised to learn that even children as young as age two can begin to take steps to understand and control their asthma. Growing up with a feeling of control and the ability to make changes and see results is powerful. It makes a difference in how patients feel emotionally and physically.

What You Have Taught Your Child with Proactive Asthma Care

So what exactly have you taught your child by practicing proactive asthma care? What have you done to begin to develop a sense of empowerment in your child, that is, to begin raising an "empowered patient"?

• **You became educated.** You and your child learned about the disease.

• **You got specific.** You focused on her condition and learned about her specific risk factors (why she was susceptible to developing asthma in the first place) and asthma triggers.

• **You got wise.** You learned about myths, stereotyping, and misinformation about asthma (including the mistaken belief that having asthma means having symptoms).

• **You focused on your goals.** You formulated specific asthma goals and discussed them with your physician, using the Childhood Asthma Bill of Rights.

• **You cultivated support from others.** You created and led a team—which included your child—to help you help her at school and elsewhere.

• **You questioned.** You learned how to raise questions and concerns with your physician; to push for the information, tests, and treatment approaches that would significantly minimize symptoms; and to better navigate the health care system (regarding insurance and duplicate prescriptions for medication, devices, and so on).

- **You planned ahead.** You refused to let things slide and learned how to quickly and efficiently put your asthma management plan in place while traveling, at camp, and elsewhere.
- **You grew assertive and gained confidence.** You put the health of your child first and asked in advance about environments that could provoke symptoms—from birthday parties to sleepovers.
- **You reviewed, assessed, and made changes.** You continually assessed your child's progress against measurable and realistic criteria (the Childhood Asthma Bill of Rights) and made decisions (including switching physicians), if necessary.

In short, you taught by example, involving your child and giving her a template on which to develop her own empowerment skills. Through you, she began to learn how to make decisions to safeguard her own health, learning about triggers and speaking up when necessary to avoid having an asthma episode.

The Asthma Care Training (A.C.T.) for Kids

Having built this strong foundation, you will want to continue cultivating your child's patient empowerment skills. Several colleagues and I developed the Asthma Care Training (A.C.T.) for Kids to help children gain skills in self-managing asthma in a way that is engaging and interactive. Designed for children age seven through twelve, the program is delivered over the course of three sessions, each ninety minutes long. Children are preferably taught by an elementary school teacher, and parents by a health care professional, typically a nurse or pharmacist. In this program, you and your child will, in separate classrooms, learn more about living with and managing asthma and then come together at the end of each session to discuss what you learned.

A.C.T. focuses on teaching children to work with their parents, health care professionals, and physicians to enhance their ability to make decisions that will help them live symptom-free lives. The program provides specific exercises to help them learn how to communicate with adults, and it reviews how to avoid triggers, prevent symptoms, and properly use medications.

A detailed overview of A.C.T. for Kids and its benefits is available at the website of the Asthma and Allergy Foundation of America (www.aafa.org). Your physician, nurse, or local pharmacist might welcome the opportunity to assist parents in the community raising children with asthma and appreciate your assistance in putting an A.C.T. program together in your area. The skills learned in A.C.T. have been shown to have a lasting impact on children and their parents.

Enjoying a Symptom-Free Future

Asthma, as we've learned, is a chronic and very unpredictable disease. Being symptom-free does not mean that the disease has disappeared. Many people believe that it "goes away," requiring less attention than it did in childhood. Indeed, some children do experience what may look like a remission in adolescence. But in general, when you stop monitoring with your peak-flow meter, stop visiting the physician at least once every six months, and abandon treatment and trigger control, the asthma may come back with equal severity.

More than half of all people (except for those with very mild asthma) require some daily asthma medication through adolescence and into adulthood. Once asthma is stabilized, there is no need to take daily peak-flow readings, but your child should resume monitoring whenever she develops cold symptoms, begins to cough, changes her medication regimen or doses, or experiences a change in her environment. She should also monitor every day during the week before a physician office visit, so that her airway status can be reviewed with her physician.

No doubt, newer and better asthma treatments will become available, and you and your child will want to explore with your doctor whether they may be right for her. However, I don't envision a cure any time soon, so asthma will need to be followed and treated into the foreseeable future. Despite the need for control and medication, however, your child need not be hampered. Using her tools of empowerment and the basics of proactive asthma care, she can look forward to a full and active life. Specifically, she will need to continue to educate herself and others about asthma, stick with an asthma treatment plan, and plan ahead—especially when confronting a major physical or environmental change.

As you may have noticed, a cornerstone of asthma management is the establishment and reliance on routines. Life milestones, however exciting, can be disruptive and wreak havoc on routines and schedules. As a result, they can have a significant impact on an individual's asthma and can often find people once again struggling with daily symptoms. Here are some life situations that could prompt a return to asthma symptoms, along with tips on how to steer clear of potential problems.

Asthma at College

For most young adults, the transition from high school to college is monumental, completely altering daily routine, social patterns, and how and where they live. Most notably, they move from a teenage life under the supervision of their parents to one of semi-independence. The peer pressures from high school continue, only now they are exacerbated by an increasing sense of invincibility.

Young adults are notorious for eschewing health habits, in large measure because their life stage makes it difficult for them to see the potentially negative consequences of their actions. Their familiar high school routines are replaced with inadequate sleep, junk food, exposure to cigarette smoke, and the unfortunate use of illegal drugs and alcohol—taking the place of parent-supervised eating and social habits. All of this change invariably contributes to stress, anxiety, depression, and other emotional ups and downs, which can provoke symptoms and also make it less likely that your child will keep to an asthma management plan.

Even with good adherence, a dormitory environment is far from asthma-friendly. Proximity to other students increases your child's risk of respiratory infections, and the dorms themselves are often old and damp, teeming with mold and dust mites. Before these challenges cause you and your young adult to consider college a lost cause, it is critical that you remember the steps for managing asthma at school, as they help you with your child's asthma management plan for college.

Regardless of the internal pull to sideline asthma control, your young adult will have a terrible college experience if her asthma symptoms are out of control. It's that simple. Asthma symptoms can make life unbearable, and if her asthma problems return, she will not be able to enjoy her college experience to its fullest. Moreover, her academic performance will suffer as well.

There is no mistaking that controlling asthma at college can be a challenge. But your empowered young adult should be able to take steps, with your help, to ensure that her asthma doesn't interfere with her new college life. With your support and guidance, she can use the following tips for preparing for and living at college:

- Try to get a single dormitory room or, at minimum, a nonsmoking roommate.
- If possible, discuss with her roommate in advance the use of a room air filter or dehumidifier or humidifier.
- Plan a visit to the physician to discuss any adjustments to medication or the asthma management plan.
- Take to college two copies of the asthma medical records— one for your child, the other for student health services.
- Determine the nearest emergency department and how to get there.
- Ask for the names of asthma or allergy specialists in the college town, in case she needs to see one during the school year.
- Distribute and discuss the asthma management plan when you arrive. Make sure your child gives a copy to her roommate, resident assistant, and hall director.
- Encourage your child to do all she can to avoid trigger situations, including environments where people smoke.
- If she has food allergies, discuss together how best to approach the school dining hall director, roommates, and friends about her food allergies and about the roommates and friends not eating foods she is allergic to in her room. Also, remind her to carry her Epi-pen at all times and exercise caution when eating out or at the college dining hall, as cross contamination does occur.
- If your child is sensitive to dust mites, make sure that she takes her pillow and mattress cover when she moves into the dorm. Remind her to wash bed linens weekly in hot water. (Discourage carpets and upholstered furniture, and remind

her to keep her dorm room as dust-free as possible—as difficult as that might be.)

Asthma on the Job

There are very few occupations that your child should not consider, but several are known to increase asthma symptoms or episodes. While you may feel it is too early to consider the topic, I think it's a good idea to spend some time reviewing the most problematic occupations early on. Understandably, parents focus their energies on the here and now when it comes to asthma, and that makes sense. But I am continually struck by the lack of questions I get with regard to the future. I don't suggest overplanning for years to come, but some thought should be given to the implications of asthma in adulthood. There are certain lines of work that could pose problems, and both of you should know about them. When the time comes to consider jobs and careers, you both can review alternatives.

Not surprisingly, the occupations that are known to exacerbate symptoms are those that would place her in an environment loaded with asthma triggers. These are environments that require that people use or breathe in chemical fumes or smoke, handle food, or work with animals. Even asthmatics without an allergy to animals in childhood will develop one if they are repeatedly exposed later in life. Having asthma and allergies makes you vulnerable to allergies in general, so a career as a zoologist or veterinarian should probably be avoided. Jobs requiring contact with chemicals could prove difficult for any person with asthma, as most people with the disease would begin to experience symptoms if inhaling fumes or vapors every day. A career as a bartender may also be impossible for someone with asthma who simply could not contend with the cigarette smoke. Other occupations that would require careful consideration and/or should be avoided include:

- Laboratory workers
- Chemical workers
- Farmers/growers
- Food processors
- Carpenters, woodworkers

- Printers
- Health care workers/pharmaceutical manufacturing workers
- Electrical workers
- Metal workers/joiners/locksmiths
- Tanners/textile workers
- Hairdressers

Special Issues for Girls

Boys outnumber girls with asthma by nearly two to one, and their asthma flares are more frequent and serious—until puberty. Then, for reasons we don't completely understand, the statistics on gender turn upside down. Following puberty, girls with asthma experience the same rate of episodes as boys, and in adulthood, the risks to women increase. More girls than boys are likely to develop asthma in adolescence and adulthood, making it more prevalent in women than in men. The latest statistics show that of the 17 million cases of asthma in the United States, 55 percent of those are in women.

If you have a daughter and a son with asthma, you may have noticed that her asthma episodes are less severe, which could lead to a false sense of security as she grows older. However, we find that puberty is the point at which girls' asthma symptoms grow worse. Far from easing up, you and she should become more attentive to her symptoms, particularly around the time of menstruation.

While the data are inconclusive, there is evidence linking the hormonal changes of the menstrual cycle to an increase in asthma symptoms and episodes, suggesting that drops in estrogen at the start of the menstrual period may make the airways more sensitive to triggers and allergens. There may also be some connection to the use of over-the-counter pain relievers such as ibuprofen, which is often used to alleviate menstrual cramps. Such medications are known to increase asthma symptoms in some patients.

When your daughter begins to menstruate, she may find that she experiences symptoms on the first day of the menstrual period, when estrogen levels are at their lowest. It is important to note any patterns and discuss them with her physician. Your physician should communicate the need for ongoing attention to her asthma throughout her life. Once in puberty, females not only experience more serious asthma symptoms than males, but their asthma episodes around menstruation can be severe.

Asthma will also be a factor when she decides to have children. Asthma is the most common medical complication of pregnancy and can be extremely unpredictable. One-third of all women with asthma will experience a reduction in symptoms, one-third will stay the same, and in the remaining third, their symptoms will grow worse. There is no way to know what kind of experience awaits her. If your daughter is still young, there may be no reason to broach the subject now. But at some point in adolescence, she should have a basic awareness of the issue of asthma in pregnancy and that, when the time comes—provided she is particularly careful to control triggers and follow her asthma management plan—she can look forward to a normal pregnancy and a healthy baby.

Concluding Remarks

THIS BOOK, INDEED, my thirty-year practice, has rested on an essential premise: that every child, in fact, any person with asthma is entitled to a healthy, active life in which choices are not overly determined by the asthma. Regardless of the severity of asthma, the specific triggers and allergens, the family's socioeconomic circumstances, and the family's beliefs about illness and well-being, every person with asthma can achieve freedom from symptoms. Certainly, there are differences—cultural, financial, and personal—but I've never viewed those differences as impediments to health and well-being.

Proactive asthma care and the four-week plan can be implemented anywhere by virtually any parent and child. It doesn't require that a parent have access to top-flight specialists at prestigious medical centers, and it doesn't require that adults or children have outgoing, assertive personalities or some special awareness and perception of themselves or the medical community. In fact, this approach was designed for everyone else.

It only requires that you accept the realities of childhood asthma and make a commitment to doing what is necessary to gain control of your child's asthma symptoms. If you've been on the four-week journey, then you've joined the thousands of parents and patients from my practice who live with few, if any, asthma symptoms. In my experience, it is that commitment that not only helped your child improve but also instilled in both of you the confidence, resilience, and determination that will enable both of you to clear asthma's hurdles and shape a satisfying, unencumbered, self-determined future.

Resources

Resources for Parents

Allergy and Asthma Network/Mothers of Asthmatics
2751 Prosperity Ave., #150
Fairfax, VA 22031
800-878-4403
www.aanma.org

American Academy of Allergy, Asthma and Immunology
555 E. Wells St.
Milwaukee, WI 53202
800-822-2762
www.aaaai.org

American Academy of Pediatrics
141 Northwest Point Blvd.
Elk Grove Village, IL 60007
847-434-4000
www.aap.org

American College of Allergy, Asthma and Immunology
85 W. Algonquin Rd., #550
Arlington Heights, IL 60005
800-842-7777
www.acaai.org

American Lung Association
800-LUNG-USA
www.lungusa.org

American Thoracic Society
61 Broadway
New York, NY 10006
www.thoracic.org

Asthma and Allergy Foundation of America
1233 20th St., NW
Washington, DC 20036
800-727-8462
www.aafa.org

Healthy Kids: The Key to Basics
Educational Planning for Students with Asthma and
    Other Chronic Health Conditions
79 Elmore St.
Newton, MA 02159
617-965-9637
www.healthy-kids.info/index.lasso

National Asthma Education and Prevention Program
NHLBI Information Center
PO Box 30105
Bethesda, MD 20824
301-592-8573
www.nhlbi.nih.gov

U.S. Environmental Protection Agency
Indoor Environments Division
401 M St., SW
Washington, DC 20460
800-438-4318
www.epa.gov

Resources for Children

Asthma Explorer's Club
Child Dynamics Research and Charitable Foundation
asthmaeclub@aol.com
www.asthmaeclub.com

Quest for the Code (Starbright asthma CD-ROM game)
Starlight Starbright Children's Foundation
800-315-2580
www.starbright.org

Index

About the Authors

GARY RACHELEFSKY, M.D., past president of the American Academy of Allergy, Asthma and Immunology (AAAAI), is clinical professor and associate director of the Allergy/Immunology Training Program at the Medical School in the Department of Pediatrics at UCLA School of Medicine.

Dr. Rachelefsky is director of the Allergy Research Foundation, Inc., and president of the Respiratory and Allergic Disease Foundation and has been a principal investigator of multiple clinical trials involving pharmacological agents to treat or prevent allergic rhinitis, sinusitis, asthma, and urticaria (hives).

He is a member of the board of advisors of *Parents* magazine and a member of the board of directors of the Starlight Starbright Children's Foundation. He is also author or coauthor of more than 100 peer-reviewed publications on allergy, respiratory disorders, and immunology. Dr. Rachelefsky is currently on the editorial boards of *Pediatric Allergy and Immunology*, *Pediatric Pulmonology*, and *Infectious Diseases in Children* and has been on the editorial boards of the *Journal of Allergy and Clinical Immunology*, and *Pediatrics*. His most recent research has been on the pathogenesis and treatment of sinusitis; asthma's link with allergy; the education, self-management, and pharmacological intervention in asthma; and the diagnosis and treatment of rhinitis. He has had articles published in the *Journal of*

Allergy and Clinical Immunology, Pediatrics, Journal of Pediatrics, and *Annals of Allergy and Clinical Immunology.*

Serving as the American Academy of Pediatrics' representative to the National Heart, Lung, and Blood Institute's National Asthma Education and Prevention Program, Dr. Rachelefsky has been instrumental in the development of national and international guidelines for the diagnosis and management of asthma. He is a former member and chairperson of the Conjoint Board of Allergy and Immunology, cochaired the AAAAI Pediatric Asthma Initiative, and cochaired the AAAAI Task Force on Allergic Disorders. He has been national program director of a Robert Wood Johnson initiative—Managing Pediatric Asthma: Emergency Department Demonstration Program Focusing on Childhood Asthma.

A graduate of Columbia College in New York, Dr. Rachelefsky received the Doctor of Medicine degree at Washington University in Saint Louis. He completed his medical internship at Bellevue Hospital in New York and his residency in pediatrics at Johns Hopkins Hospital in Baltimore. After completing a two-year epidemiology program at the Centers for Disease Control in Atlanta, Dr. Rachelefsky performed his fellowship in allergy and immunology at UCLA.

Patricia Garrison is a health care writer, editor, and former journalist who has written numerous consumer and medical articles, patient education materials, and white papers on the topic of allergic disease and asthma. Ms. Garrison was active in a national campaign to promote the first stand-alone guidelines for childhood asthma diagnosis and treatment addressed to the primary-care physician and pediatrician, and she has written extensively on the consequences of undiagnosed and untreated allergies and asthma and the physician-patient relationship.